Praise for ·

Reclaiming the Commons for the Common Good

It's an admirable, even noble, vision, and expresses very eloquently what will have to be done if humanity is to escape the current race towards disaster. There's not much time, and it's a huge task. I hope that this book has the impact it deserves.

—Noam Chomsky, linguist, philosopher, political theorist, MIT

When the great Crash, ecologic or economic, comes, Heather Menzies' brilliant critique, provides an understanding of why it came about and a path towards a truly sustainable way for humanity to live on the planet.

—David Suzuki, author, *Wisdom of the Elders* and *The Sacred Balance*

A book made for today. Menzies marks the trail for deep participation in the healing of soul, community and creation, drawing from ancient wisdom, fine scholarship and contemporary practices of hope. An inspiring and pragmatic contribution toward meeting the greatest spiritual challenges of our time.

—Mardi Tindal, former moderator, United Church of Canada

This is a splendid, lyrical book— exciting, well-written, scholarly and inspirational all at once ... Grounded in practical experience and sound scholarship, this book is a welcome addition to commons literature.

—Susan J. Buck, Ph.D., past president,
International Association for the Study of the Commons (IASC),
Associate Professor of Political Science,
University of North Carolina - Greensboro

The constitutional principle of compelling national interest that is invoked by governments to ensure progress and development has invariably been at the expense of local-communities and local environments. As a result, the fabric of reality is damaged and torn. This damage and tearing is known by many names and phrases; climate change, war, genocide, colonization, environmental degradation, and perhaps most appropriately as the tragedy of the commons. *Reclaiming the Commons for the Common Good* represents, for me, a first baby-step toward repairing the breach to wholeness and toward restoring ancient pathways supported both by a scientific theory of common ancestry and indigenous story of creation held-in-common.

—Eugene Richard Atleo (Umeek)

Like most thoughtful post-2008 observers, Menzies is a trenchant critic of the neoliberal version of capitalism for its destruction of community life, degradation of the environment and accelerating inequality. Unlike most, however, she presents a seamlessly argued alternative vision. Drawing on her Scottish roots, Aboriginal history, current movements like Idle No More, environmental and social justice activist practices in many countries, and Google-friendly networks, she calls upon individuals to change the world by engaging locally within this complex matrix. She contends that it's possible, if not easy, to re-establish communities whose prevailing ethic is the common good. This would allow for markets; but instead of continuing to dominate, they would be subordinated to society's local and national priorities. A powerful challenge to the to the still prevailing ideology.

—Ed Broadbent, chair, Broadbent Institute, and former leader,
New Democratic Party of Canada

Reclaiming the Commons for the Common Good

A Memoir & Manifesto

HEATHER MENZIES

new society
PUBLISHERS

Cover design by Diane McIntosh.

Cover image: A grazing common land behind Ben Lawrs in the Tay River Valley of Scotland where Heather's ancestors would have pastured their sheep and cows for the summer. Photo: Heather Menzies

Printed in Canada. First printing March 2014.

New Society Publishers acknowledges the financial support of the Government of Canada through the Canada Book Fund (CBF) for our publishing activities.

Paperback ISBN: 978-0-86571-758-9
eISBN: 978-1-55092-558-6

Inquiries regarding requests to reprint all or part of *Reclaiming the Commons for the Common Good* should be addressed to New Society Publishers at the address below.

To order directly from the publishers, please call toll-free (North America) 1-800-567-6772, or order online at www.newsociety.com

Any other inquiries can be directed by mail to:

New Society Publishers
P.O. Box 189, Gabriola Island, BC V0R 1X0, Canada
(250) 247-9737

New Society Publishers' mission is to publish books that contribute in fundamental ways to building an ecologically sustainable and just society, and to do so with the least possible impact on the environment, in a manner that models this vision. We are committed to doing this not just through education, but through action. The interior pages of our bound books are printed on Forest Stewardship Council®-registered acid-free paper that is **100% post-consumer recycled** (100% old growth forest-free), processed chlorine-free, and printed with vegetable-based, low-VOC inks, with covers produced using FSC®-registered stock. New Society also works to reduce its carbon footprint, and purchases carbon offsets based on an annual audit to ensure a carbon neutral footprint. For further information, or to browse our full list of books and purchase securely, visit our website at: www.newsociety.com

Library and Archives Canada Cataloguing in Publication

Menzies, Heather, 1949-, author
    Reclaiming the commons for the common good : a memoir & manifesto /
Heather Menzies.

Includes bibliographical references and index.
Issued in print and electronic formats
ISBN 978-0-86571-758-9 (pbk.).—ISBN 978-1-55092-558-6 (ebook)

    1. Commons—Scotland—Highlands. 2. Commons—Anecdotes.
3. Highlands (Scotland)—Biography. 4. Highlands (Scotland)—Description and travel.
5. Menzies, Heather, 1949-. 6. Menzies, Heather, 1949- —Family.
7. Menzies, Heather, 1949-—Travel—Scotland—Highlands. 8. Authors,
Canadian (English)—20th century—Biography. I. Title.

HD1289.S35M45 2014   333.209411'5   C2014-900432-X
                                                    C2014-900433-8

For all our relations, human and non-human,
and the ancestral spirits that sustain them,
in loving memory of my father, Donald Menzies,
and what he had inscribed on a rock,
and for my son, Donald, with love

Contents

Part III: *Reclaiming the Commons — a Manifesto*

Preface

*I*GREW UP ON PHRASES LIKE 'COMMON AS DIRT.' *When I was young and eager to go out on dates, my mother warned me to be careful lest I be considered common, meaning cheap, available, readily used and then discarded. I didn't know that 'common' originally meant a way of living on the land. Nor did I know that my ancestors in the Highlands of Scotland lived that way, in self-governing commons where they farmed and pastured their sheep together. The word common originally meant 'together-as-one,' 'shared alike' and 'bound together by obligation.' This togetherness was not only with each other, but with the land itself.*

It's time to reclaim the commons, first as memory and heritage and then as practices and the capacity to once again live together-as-one with the Earth.

Introduction

A T A TIME OF FEELING AT A DEAD END, I went to Scotland looking for my ancestral and even, I hoped, my tribal roots. In the rugged glens of the Tay River Valley, I discovered a legacy of which I had known nothing: a people, my people, living in direct relations with the land in self-governing commons and commons communities, small villages or hamlets called *fermtouns* or *townships*. They set *stints*, or limits, on the number of sheep and cows to be sent to the upland common pasture, and decided how often field strips should be left to rest, to lie fallow and recover their fertility. The legacy I discovered included great loss as well: a loss that goes well beyond the dislocation of people from the land itself through the Highland clearances. My ancestors weren't just displaced. They were dispossessed. They were stripped of their traditional knowledge vested in the land, their ways of knowing through the experience of working that land, their ways of sharing this in a commons of knowledge and, in their spiritual practices, honoring their place in Creation. They were disenfranchised too because they lost the legitimacy of local self-governance, the local interpretation of justice, fairness and the common good. The so-called tragedy of the commons, I learned as I explored this lost history, turns out to have been based not on the facts of how people like my ancestors lived on the land but on assumptions useful to those trying to clear them off of it.

Belatedly, awkwardly, I mourned that loss and owned it. Then I boarded my flight home. Even on the plane, way up there at cruising altitude, I knew that I'd crossed some threshold. I grew up with my hands in the dirt, in the backyard of our home in a postwar suburb of Montreal and at our family farm in Eastern Ontario, Canada. There, I'd planted trees, picked stones from the fields, plowed and even helped pull weeds, acres at a stretch, by hand. I've continued growing a vegetable garden every summer of my adult life, freezing and preserving to have a store of chemical-free food with which to feed my family. But having walked the land with which my forbears had lived in direct and possibly even right relations since before recorded time and having done some important memory work, I felt connected to the Earth in a way I never had before. It was as though the center of my inner gravity had shifted. The intellectual fact that the word human derives from humus, the fecund soil of the Earth, began to resonate with a deeper, felt meaning. Not quite kinship, but moving in that direction. As I left the airport that day, I knew I was onto something important.

I have stepped outside the box of modernity and stepped into a place where my First Nations neighbors no longer seem alien, exotic and totally different from me. As I watch them recover their lost traditions, renew their old practices and relearn their mother tongues, as I watch individuals I know struggle on their journeys of recovery, I sense parallels in the journey that so-called settlers in North America like me can undertake, personally and collectively, and perhaps need to as well.[1]

My journey gave me a precious new perspective for this, one of those Archimedean places to stand from which to change the world. The self-governing common is an economic and political institution that, according to some vindicating research by Nobel-prize winning economist Elinor Ostrom, continues to represent a viable alternative to the market or the state as a core regulator of society. Historically, though, the commons was more than that. It was a community in the fullest sense of the word, and an ecological one as well. The word *common* originally meant together-as-one, or together-in-one (see Glossary), with both the land and the people inhabiting it included in that togetherness. *Commoning* — cultivating community and livelihood together on the common land of the Earth — was a way of life for my ancestors and for many other newcomers to North America too. It was a way of understanding and pursuing economics as embedded in life and the labor, human and non-human, that is necessary to sustain it. It was a way of ordering this life through local self-governance and direct, participatory democracy. And it was a way of knowing, through doing and the sharing of experience through common knowledge and common sense. This commons shaped people's identity, through its web work of commoning relationships that spun themselves afresh each day through the sharing of work, stories and faith rituals, through struggle over differences and working things out together. The commoners who were my ancestors were no doubt individuals, with all the normal inclinations toward greed, spite and self-interest. They were also immersed in the rhythms of ongoing connection, of mutual obligation, mutual self-interest and quotidian lessons on the common good.

I've spent my adult life watching the scope for common ground and the common good slip away with both the loss of community locally and the withering of the social welfare state. I have also watched, and written about, the ascendency of market forces in all areas of life, including the care of seniors. I have witnessed a matching rise of dependency: dependency on jobs, on investment and credit, on credentials to act. Even at the level of knowledge to leverage change from an increasingly unworkable status quo, ordinary people seem to require numbers and experts to convince official policy makers to do something, be it about climate change or the toxic injustices of the global economy. Control has been concentrated into the hands of a small elite, not just in investment markets and global corporations, but in the research and regulatory bodies, including the World Trade Organization, that support this elite. Here we clearly see the realm of the 1 or 2% who control an estimated 60% of everything. The effect of that control can be called colonization and dependency when viewed politically. When viewed sociologically and psychologically, it could also be called conditioning for compliance with the status quo. Culturally, concentration of control has narrowed the vision of perceived alternatives and silenced any language for even considering them. As a writer, teacher and conference speaker, I have critiqued all this and tried to name the impasse it has produced. On the one hand, an overextended and increasingly dysfunctional global market economy is on a collision course with an overheated and increasingly damaged Earth. On the other, a combination of gridlocked vested interests and the lack of an alternative on which people can get a real grip keeps things stuck in the status quo. In North America, the only recourse has been protest. It flares up, touching people's deep-seated anxiety and their longing for meaningful change, and then seems to fade away. Protest seems to sometimes be all people feel capable of too, or have time for in their busy, often debt-burdened lives.

The legacy of the commons offers a way out of this impasse. It offers a model of society that is centered in people's relationships with each other and with the land, not in remote state authorities or an anonymous market. It offers a healing ethos of connection, not disconnection, of implicated participation, not remote control and management.

Some of these practices operate on a personal level, some at a more institutional level and some at a more political level still. Yet they're all of a piece. They all work together. Change must happen at every level of existence from the personal to the institutional and the political. It's through practices that a commoning ethos can be restored. A consciousness that has all but disappeared in the non-native community can surface again: a consciousness of our connection to the Earth.

I was there on December 21, 2012 when the Idle No More Movement marched on Parliament Hill in Ottawa, Canada and a regional chief spoke of a "sacred covenant with Creation" having been broken by the Harper Government's omnibus legislation cutting regulation and custodial oversight of the environment. I was on Victoria Island on January 6, 2013 when a man identifying himself as a seventh generation descendent of Chief Tecumseh (who led a First Nations alliance with the British in the War of 1812) visited Chief Theresa

Spence during the hunger strike she undertook as her own Idle No More initiative. I watched as he stood on one side of the sacred fire, Tecumseh's flag in one hand and told Chief Spence: "You speak from the heart of the Earth." And I was on Parliament Hill again on January 28, 2013 for another Idle No More protest where a young member of the Indigenous Environmental Network talked of "our sacred responsibility" to speak for the fish being poisoned by the seepage from Tar Sands tailing ponds.

Listening to those words, I heard a language that's virtually died out of public discourse and policy debate in Canada. I also recognized it as the language that must be revived if those of us who care for life on Earth and want a better future for our children are to break out of this impasse. It's a language of empathy and engagement, of mutual recognition, respect and implicated participation. It's the language of relationships and felt connection with each other and with the Earth.

Reviving this language, and the practices associated with it, is key to enacting a new social contract, one that includes a new covenant with Creation. The heritage of the commons, which so many so-called non-natives have in their ancestral past, is a way for such people, including me, to revive that language among ourselves. It's the language of relationships and felt connection with each other and with the Earth.

As a fifth-generation settler immigrant to North America, this heritage is what I can offer to the work of renewal that is going on in all its varied forms: common cause alliances among environmental, social justice, faith and First Nations communities around their specific goals of local self-governance and fulfilling treaty obligations; community-based healing and support, including local food and housing initiatives, for those displaced from the global market economy, or too sick to survive in its frenzy of competition and constant change; initiatives addressing toxins in the natural environment and change-agent activists trying to mitigate and reverse the forces of climate change. I hope that the commons, and its ethos of commoning with each other and with the Earth, might even act as a frame for integrating and building on some of these alternatives.

Drawing on the legacy of the commons, I invite people to come home to themselves, come home to community as habitat and to the Earth as the larger habitat in which all life is nested. I also encourage people to take seriously their own knowing and local knowledge derived from implicated engagement in all the habitats in which their lives are immersed. I suggest ways to engage with the Earth in places where people currently live, and ways to build or rebuild the capacity for self-determination and responsible self-governance within those habitats.

I came of age under banner slogans like "reclaim the power of naming" and "the personal is political," and I bring the legacy of that to what I've written here. I speak in a personal voice as an implicated participant in my own life and the habitats in which I have dwelled, while also drawing on material I've researched. I also move back and forth between the more political language of capacity and institution building and the more intimate language of healing and personal growth. To me, a mixed perspective and language is necessary and mutually reinforcing. If we are to reconnect with the Earth and find the will to halt the environmental devastation of our time, both social and natural, we must also reconnect with ourselves and with each other.

The first part of the book is a road trip, a summary of my efforts to reconnect with a lost heritage of my ancestors in the Highlands of Scotland. The second part interprets the significance of what I discovered and identifies different forms of capacity building that the commons legacy can inspire and inform. The third part moves from capacity to action. Here I offer what I cheekily call a Commoning Manifesto, a brief sketch of what we might do, drawing in examples of initiatives going on right now that I see as fitting into a commoning framework.

The Indian writer Arundhati Roy told the 2003 World Social Forum that not only is another world possible, but is on her way, and that on a quiet day you can hear her breathing.[2] That breath could include the spirits of our ancestors calling to us, ready to inspire and guide us, as we open our hearts and listen.

Part I

Reclaiming the Commons as Memory

At an Impasse

I WAS FEELING STUCK AT THE TIME I FIRST WENT TO SCOTLAND because I'd run out of things to say. I had been writing about market globalization and the shift to an online world, critiquing the disconnect from self, others and community, the deepening inequalities and the desperate dependency on jobs, jobs jobs, as well as the brave new Darwinism of speed and outperformance. More recently, I had linked this shift with the disaster of environmental degradation and global warming, seeing them as mutually reinforcing: an overextended global economy and an overheated planet. Yet I could offer nothing by way of real alternatives. I knew what I was against, but not what I was FOR. Or rather, I couldn't name any alternative or feel it in a way that I could get a real grip on, strong and real enough to inspire action, action that could be sustained through a movement for genuine change.

I was haunted by an image I'd encountered in a 1989 book, called *Technology as Symptom and Dream*, by American psychologist Robert Romanyshyn.[1] He used the astronaut in outer space as a metaphor for the dream embedded in modern technology and the pursuit of it — the dream of limitless freedom and control. He contrasted this image with the anorexic body, abandoned in that pursuit of control. The astronaut image has stayed with me because I see it playing itself out so clearly in today's wireless world. So many of us are out there doing our own space walks, each with a miniaturized life-support system built into our space suits (our screen masks, handhelds and earbuds allowing us to be anywhere anytime). It's total freedom far removed from Earth's gravitational pull, while tethered to a space station in an orbit all its own — the space station being the global digital economy perhaps?

I was reminded of Romanyshyn's imagery when reading Richard Louv's 2008 book, *Last Child in the Woods*, chronicling what he calls a nature deficit disorder in children growing up today, cut off from opportunities to simply be in nature. "Containerized kids" Louv called them.[2] Astronauts in training, I thought when I read this. But where was I in all this? I wasn't healing the deficit, the disparities or the disconnect. In the way I was writing, in the way I had been trained to write if I wanted to be taken seriously in the public arenas of discussion, I felt like I myself was an astronaut or perhaps on the space station itself. I was always removed from the situation, offering fix-it suggestions from my position as "expert" at the master controls. I wasn't grounded in real life, real people's bodies or the lived social environment. I wasn't implicated or engaged, nor could I be if I wanted to maintain my "objectivity" and therefore my credibility and my place at official (and well-funded) debates.

It was the same with other critics, I found. In book after book, whether critiquing the global economy and the financialization of everything or chronicling its effects in climate change and environmental collapse, the language and tone were similar: so remote it was as though the disasters were happening on another planet. No wonder no real alternatives were emerging. I was part of the impasse. I needed to break out of it, but how?

A few years earlier, I had accepted an invitation to join a native women's drumming and chanting circle that met once a week at Minwaashin Lodge near the Ottawa bus station. One day when women were introducing themselves, saying their spirit name, then naming their clan and tribal connections, I said that one day I hoped to find out more about my own tribal roots, which I knew were in the Highlands of Scotland,

and bring back what I learned to this circle. The women had been so welcoming, so generous in sharing their traditions, their still-living heritage, and I wanted to reciprocate. I didn't know what looking for my tribal roots might entail, nor what I had in mind when I spoke my intention. But I could feel the call as soon as I'd uttered those words, and now, nearly four years later, I heeded it.

As I packed and prepared myself, I told my friends that I wanted to walk the land where my ancestral roots lay buried, not to learn details about my genealogy so much as to ground myself. I had a vague sense of wanting to dwell in a state of unlearning and even unknowing. I wanted to find and, if possible, set myself down in the gap where other paths and ways of being in the world had been abandoned and left to die away. These ways might whisper to me, I thought, maybe even speak to my troubled world. I sort of had in mind, though I never said so, what Canadian philosopher George Grant once referred to as "intimations of deprival."[3] These were all that remained, Grant wrote in *Technology and Empire*, when a society becomes "barren of anything but the drive to technology..." In such a society as ours has become, he continued, "the moral discourse of 'values,' is not independent of the will to technology, but a language fashioned in the same forge."[4]

When I spoke of my travel plans, most of my friends just nodded and smiled and asked no further questions. But Morning Star Woman (Bev) from the drumming circle did more than smile and nod. She chuckled as if she fully understood. "You're going to welcome your ancestors back," she said as if this was the most normal thing in the world to do.

"Yes," I said, surreptitiously writing down her words, making sure I packed this note in my bag. Because it hadn't occurred to me to even imagine such a possibility: that there might have been voices behind my sense of being called; a dialogue waiting to be renewed.

Crossing a Threshold

I WENT TO SCOTLAND THAT SPRING WITH A SINGLE CLUE, one word, to guide me. The word was Tullicro; I had no idea what it meant. It showed up in a family geneology a friend of the family had prepared, as part of the entry for my great, great grandfather James Menzies who, it said, was born in 1792, at Tullicro, Dull, near Aberfeldy in Perthshire, Scotland. I had travelled to Aberfeldy by bus from the train station at Dunkeld at one end of the Tay River Valley, and already I'd learned that Aberfeldy is derived from two Gaelic words which mean "mouth of the river spirit, a shaggy beast called Phaelle or Phaeldy."[1] In the comfort of a lovely bed-and-breakfast, I laid out my map of Scotland and found Dull easily enough, just across the tumultuous Tay River from where I was staying. I rented a bicycle to take me there and then simply asked around. It turned out that Tullicro is the name of a premodern commons community called a fermtoun or ferm township. Such settlements "formed the basic communities of Gaeldom from time immemorial, according to one historian.[2] They evolved, it seems, as clans and tribes of Neolithic hunt-er-farmers, often known simply as *tuatha* (meaning "the people"), became more settled over time.[3] The Roman historian Tacitus wrote about these common communities, describing them too as "chiefly democratic."[4] In remote Highland valleys like those of the Tay and Glen Lyon rivers, these settlements lasted into the 1800s. As one historian wrote: "Everyday life for most Scots was lived on or in some way closely connected with the land"[5] Wrote another: "Commoning was a way of life."[6]

At Dull, someone directed me to an aging local farmer who pointed a work-gnarled hand down the valley and directed me to Tullicro, explaining that remnants of this old walled settlement still existed. It stood at the top of an unpaved, potholed, tree-lined laneway that ran up the hillside so steeply I had to get off my bicycle and push. Out of breath at the top, I stopped and stared. Most of the buildings had been renovated, some even turned into tourist rentals, I learned later.

But one building looked much as it was more than a century ago. It was a traditional *crux cottage*, of longhouse construction[7] that once would have had a *byre* at one end where the cows, ducks and chickens were kept. The byre was gone, but the original roof was still there, looking shabby and worn like the rest of the place. This might have been where my great, great grandfather was born! Still breathing hard, I gazed at its still intact endwall and chimney stack made entirely of stone placed precisely on stone, with no mortar binding the stones together. I noted the low entranceway and the small inset windows. I walked toward the cottage, my eye taking in the details of its simple endurance in this place. I leaned my bike against the stone wall and looked around the weed-strewn yard. Perhaps this is where my great, great grandfather first played outside, did his share of household chores, minding the hens and chickens and, maybe, even some ducks.

At first I simply biked back again and again to Tullicro, amazed to find this threshold into a past about which I had known nothing. My people were tenant farmers, and from what I gather, hailed from clans that had inhabited this valley since Neolithic and even Mesolithic times, long before identities such as tenants and landlords were created. I learned too that the thatching on the roof was made from reeds gathered from the shores of the Tay River, reeds that were growing there still. One afternoon, I climbed over the stile and into a pasture where sheep were grazing, as they likely had nearly a thousand years. The more I walked, the more I explored, the more I felt called to come back again.

To the Shieling

Tullicro became an archeological dig site to me, a place where I could connect what I learned over the next two years from reading all I could get my hands on about the commons and the history of everyday life in the Highlands. When I returned to Scotland from Canada, I rented the smallest of the renovated buildings on the fermtoun, what had been a *bothy* (a sleeping quarters for unmarried men and hired hands). It was and still is a simple granite box of a place with two small windows on either side of the narrow, low door, the key to which is a long, iron latchkey, which scraped matching iron deep inside the thick plank of wood that was the door as I unlocked it. I moved in my stuff, and turned on the heat, glad of the mod cons that had been added with the renovation. I picked some flowers from the yard outside, weeds really, but pretty still. I took my time arranging them in a mug, set this on the table where I'd eat and work during my stay, then went to air out my bed. I took my time. I walked the fields where my ancestors had labored semi-communally, with scattered strips of the infield shared out by lots. I sussed out where old pathways, called *loans* and *driftways*,[1] which also served as common rights of way used to be. I found a stone that seemed more than just another piece of glacial erratic. It might have been a *march* or *mark stone* from the days when

Tullicro was a flourishing common. Large standing stones were used to mark the boundaries of land that was farmed in common, boundaries that my ancestors "marched" at least once every year in a ritual ceremony to ensure that no one had erected some hedging or fencing, enclosing a bit of land for private gain.[2] In one account at least, any such evidence of enclosing would be summarily destroyed, with axes and mattocks carried along for the purpose.[3]

I liked that story, the cheerful efficiency of local justice, though aware too of its shadow in the abuse of such power and its potential conflict with higher, more remote authorities as these intruded more and more over time with a different way of ordering and organizing society, and even of understanding its purpose. Still, I got in the habit of visiting the mark stone when I was out walking the fields, now a sheep pasture. If the day was sunny and warm, I sometimes clambered on top where there was a small depression and sat there, arms hugging my knees to my chest, having a good think.

A few days later, I felt bold enough to head out into the hills in search of the shielings where my people spent most of the summer — typically from Beltane to Lammas according to the old pagan calendar that was still observed for time keeping if nothing more. The word *shieling* means "enclosure in the wilderness" (wilderness being an Old English word meaning "wild deer" or the place where the wild deer roam).[4] These enclosures were sheep folds and small stone shelters (bothies) the commoners built to shelter themselves from summer storms and to store their iron cooking pots, wood and horn spoons, plus the cheeses they made over the course of the languid summer months.

I found a shieling that my ancestors likely used by scanning the detailed ordinance map for the area. It showed all the traditional footpaths through the hills, and near the dead end of one I noticed the symbol depicting the ruins of a shieling on land that had once been occupied by people of my clan. I packed food and water into my daypack and drove my small rental car along the single-lane track past Ben Lawrs to a lay-by deep enough that I could safely park it. Then I hiked into the hills, following a path that the sheep still wandering here keep nicely clear. I topped a rise and found myself on the brim of a lovely hanging valley, a bountiful stream snaking its way down the middle of it from a spot on the far side where the land rises steeply to a saddle-backed ridge. Blooming wild heather and a lingering morning mist gave the place a lavender luminosity, and I walked down the path into the valley as though I was coming home.

I found the ruins of bothies on a rise in the middle of the valley, close to a place where the stream made a turn and had formed a quiet pool. And I imagined my people coming back to them in late April and May, ready to spend the summer tending their sheep and cows, making cheese, spinning wool and weaving it into cloth and keeping the old faith practices alive; it was safe enough here in the more remote upper glens. And as they came, driving their animals before them, I imagined them singing traditional songs, many of them simply a recitation of place names, prefaced with "*Chi Mi*," meaning "I see" or "I can see." There were names for every nook and cranny of the landscape they travelled through, each with a story tucked into the Gaelic word or words for the place, stories that tradition bearers were responsible for keeping alive, stories that tied the living generation of people to the land and their ancestors who'd walked it before their time. I imagine this practice like recalling the lines of an old friend's face, a face that has been well lived in over the years. In the Highlands, the songs describe a habitat long inhabited, and known as intimately as a friend. As a 1908 account put it: "The names of hills, glades, glens, corries, streams and even pools and rapids in a river had each its legend which accounted for its origin or related some circumstance connected with it."[5]

I wandered around the ruined bothies, noting the recessed cavities and shelves contrived out of the rock at one end, noting too the droppings of a rabbit and the spot where a sheep clearly liked to lie down to sleep. I wandered over to the stream, the stone-strewn banks of which might have served as a quarry. I imagined the men hauling large rocks out of the stream bed, grabbing a chisel one of them would have forged from bog iron collected, perhaps even here, from under the peat. Using chisel and wooden mallets, they would have shaped new stones for bothies or for the walls of the enclosure where they folded the cows and sheep for milking. While the men were doing this, the women were probably off with the children gathering stalks of old heather which, bunched together, stems down and placed between the rocks or boards that framed the beds, served as mattresses for sleeping, a blanket of tartan or plain homespun serving as sheet and comforter both.

The day grew dark and the mist turned into a shower of rain, and I hunkered down in a corner of one ruin. I ate my sandwich, made from a leftover venison and cranberry sausage I'd bought from the butcher shop in Aberfeldy the previous day. The deer may have come from a "deer park" just down the road from Tullicro; I'd passed its high fences, seen the single stag stand, bellowing, on its uppermost point of land, its head with its great rack of antlers thrown back. I sat on my daypack in the corner of the broken-down bothy, nicely out of the wind and at least some of the rain. I sat there staring into the obscuring mist, using what I'd learned from my research to conjure a sense of how my people had lived here long ago, not shearing the wool but plucking it from the small Soay sheep which they would have tended here over the course of centuries since the Iron Age. I watched the present-day sheep as they grazed on the far side of the hill. Then, when the rain stopped, I walked along the paths the sheep, and perhaps long ago my ancestors too, had made, taking in the feel of the earth under my feet, the lay of the land as it sloped upward toward the far ridge. I wondered what my ancestors had called that ridge and, closer to me, the outcrop over which the stream turned into a frothing set of rapids. I drank from the stream tumbling boisterously down its age-old course, and passing a few steps away from the shieling shelters. And I opened my inner ear to the possibility of my ancestral spirits being present, whispering the old names of things to me and welcoming me back to the particular place on this planet that is my ancestral home.

I grew up walking the land at the farm my parents had bought as a weekend retreat from a Montreal suburb. I'd dug into that land, planting trees on the slopes because the farm had been abandoned in the postwar period and the soil samples came back labeled "leached, eroded, barren." I'd written about what the experience of planting thousands of trees to restore the land had meant to me in an essay republished in an anthology subtitled *Best Contemporary Canadian Nature Writing*, under the theme of "reconciliation."[6] This experience of journeying to the Highlands was more personal, a reconciliation with a past from which I'd been separated.

Perhaps it was my longing for connection. Perhaps it was the work that I'd done. From walking the land my people had walked, from immersing myself at least in the knowledge that has survived about how they lived in intimate daily connection with the land, the water, the weather as it varied through the seasons, I felt as though I was recovering something that, perhaps because of the Clearances, my great grandparents, grandparents and parents might have buried inside as too painful to remember. I caught a glimpse, a faint whisper of affiliation and myself as part of it. A continuity, a thread of connection to the land, the water and the sky of this place. I felt it tug at me, like an invisible umbilical chord. A once-lived and now remembered line of communing and communication, a continuity of connection to the Earth.

As I walked back to my rental car, it occurred to me too that this connection to the Earth is our common human heritage, the storied corollary of the word "human" deriving from humus, the soil of the Earth. Surely this heritage is in us all to reclaim and own, if we take the time to go back and open our hearts and our imaginations to what we find. Or at least that's what it seemed to be to me. Scientists today talk about how mitochondrial DNA is passed down continuously from mother to daughter, that blood flows continuously down the female line from uterus to fetus to uterus to fetus and can possibly be traced unbroken back to the beginning of humankind.[7] Why not memory — and the habits of certain practices that connect? Umbilical cords are perhaps more than meet the eye. They are metaphors to conjure with.

4

A Field in Good Heart

B Y A WEEK INTO MY STAY, I was feeling at home at Tullicro. Not exactly putting down roots, but settling in. Kevin and Jane Ramage, the couple who owned the beautifully restored cottage at the far end of the fermtoun's cluster of buildings and who run the local bookstore in Aberfeldy, the award-winning Watermill with its antique-filled café serving world-class lattes, had invited me over for a glass of wine. There, I'd met Karl Jarlow, a retired antique dealer, widowed and originally from Sweden. Karl and his wife had bought the whole of Tullicro in 1976 when all but one of its buildings were abandoned and falling apart. One by one, they had restored the buildings — the bothy was little more than waist-high rock walls with a stone floor polished from foot and animal traffic — and sold them. They'd kept the crux cottage, which was the last to be abandoned, as a place to store antiques. Karl offered to show me around inside if I liked, and the next day he did, noting the absence of plumbing and central heating as we entered the dark, low-ceilinged space. The old couple who had lived there into the 1960s were used to the old ways of coal and peat in the open-range fire in the main front room, a chain and hook for an iron cooking pot suspended from the middle of the chimney hole, a cast-iron oven on one side of the fire and a water jacket on the other. Outside, in front of the barn, Karl showed me the worn stone circle with a depression in the middle where an axle would have turned as one of the draft animals on the place, an ox or a horse, worked the quern to grind grain for the community. And in the space between the crux cottage and my bothy (what was now a parking lot fringed with a scattering of weeds) he agreed with me that, yes, this might well have been the kailyard attached to the family cottage. Potatoes, turnips and cabbage would have been grown here year after year, essential vegetables to see the family and their animals through the winter. I gazed at it fondly, imagining that my great, great grandfather might have been sent outside to weed this kailyard when he was old enough, just as my mother sent me outside to weed our vegetable garden when I was a child growing up in a postwar suburb of Montreal.

It was early September at the time, and the weeds were going to seed. So I asked Karl if I could borrow a pair of work gloves and when he graciously produced some I went to work uprooting weeds. Really, I think, I just wanted to get my hands in the dirt. I wanted to get down on my haunches and dig. Lacking tools, I used a stick and a sharp-edged stone, and soon my nose picked up the sharp smell of iron in the mix of soil and grit that came up with the roots. I remembered a line from one of the books I'd read: the local volume of the *Statistical Account of Scotland* for 1779: "The greater part of the soil is thin and gravellish,"[1] it said. Nothing's changed, I thought, as I continued digging and uprooting. Then another line surfaced — this from academic Jeanette Neeson's history of the commons that described pastures and fields as being "in good heart."[2] Through some e-mail correspondence, Neeson confirmed that the phrase was often used at the time to describe a field in good health. There was something about the phrase that intrigued me. As I sifted the dirt of Tullicro through my hands, I turned it over in my mind as though it was an artifact I'd unearthed, as telling as a broken piece of pottery. I repeated the words as I sat back on my heels looking out over this land that was my ancestral home. A field in good heart, I said aloud, dwelling on the curvature of the phrase and its trajectory, from open field to human heart. It spoke an intimacy of connection, of mutuality. Of course, my people had to maintain their fields in good health and did so, I had learned, using manure and a locally kilned limestone. By mutual agreement among their fellow commoners, they also left strips of the infield to lie fallow on a regular basis. There was utilitarian rationality at work, and yet the phrase suggested something more.

I went back to digging and, with the pointy end of a stick I'd found, I managed to get a whole plant up by the roots. I sat back, satisfied, watching the sandy soil and fine pebbles around which these roots and root hairs had nested fall to the ground. I knew from a book in the bothy that this plant was ragwort, toxic to horses. But I didn't know whether it propagated by seed or whether a single bit of root or leaf would do (as it will for portulaca, the scourge of my garden back home). My ancestors would have known, though. They'd have learned by experience, by careful observation and sharing that with others. These are old ways of knowing preserved in traditional crafts. "You go by the feel a lot," I remember an old cheese maker telling me once when he knew the curd had formed enough that it was time to run off the whey. It's attuned attention, a way of knowing through intimate engagement. Then, thinking once again of that phrase "a field in good heart," it occurred to me: perhaps my ancestors knew their fields by heart. I laughed at the thought, even while rejecting such sentimentality, and chucked the ragwort into my weed bucket.

I sat back on my heels and just squatted there for a while, taking in the earth smell, the plant smell, the freshness of the autumn air. I poked the ground with my stick, picking out stones much as I had as a kid at the farm every spring. I took off a glove and gathered a handful of gravelly dirt into my hand. I squeezed it, feeling it cohere, if barely, into a lump. Then I raised my fisted hand to my chest, remembering another finding from my research. In some communities, when an individual who'd been elected to act as juror or field constable for the common took up his duties, he did so in a ritual that involved picking up a handful of soil and holding it to his heart. Sometimes, he took off his hat and his shoes and stockings too, making direct bodily contact with the Earth. Then with a fistful of dirt held to his chest, he made his pledge: "*am fianuis uir agus adhair am fianus De agus daoine*" (in the witness of my father, and in witness of God and man) that he would be faithful to his trust: to serve both the land and the people who labored it in the local commons settlement.[3]

I brushed the dirt off my hand, then whacked Karl's work gloves against my leg. They had been clean and seemingly brand new when I borrowed them. Now they were creased in the palm and stained from the earth — a faint reminder of my presence in them, of my brief time of laboring this land. Yes, I thought as I returned to the bothy to make a cup of tea, these phrases are scant evidence and faded at that; yet surely they suggest an ethos of connection that I can claim as my heritage, and have even felt faintly all my life as I've worked in the garden, planted trees at the farm and hiked in hills and mountains.

Curiously, connecting or reconnecting with the Earth illuminates some of the new philosophy that's emerged from quantum physics. As people like Fritjof Capra, author of *The Turning Point* and *The Tao of Physics*, have written, the revelations associated with Einstein's work on relativity teach us that everything is connected to everything else. There's no such thing as free-floating individual atoms and laws of motion (or supply and demand) that operate independently, as laws unto themselves. That's fiction. Matter dances in infinite interconnection there to be sensed, respected and worked with.[4] Still, grasping this intellectually is one thing. It's quite another to recognize it like a long-lost piece of family history — like something retrieved from an old family trunk in the attic, a garment you can slip on and find that it even seems to fit. Connection is central to these old ways of living and knowing what to do, attuned to how everything relates to everything else.

Duthchas and the Ethos of the Commons

DUTHCHAS OR DUALCHAS WAS ANOTHER OF MY ARCHAEOLOG-ICAL FINDS, another artifact that I could conjure with, turning it over in my mind. The word translates from the Gaelic as what most people today would simply call one's heritage. In premodern Scotland, it meant much more than that. It was a lived set of rights and also responsibilities toward one's family and the land that they inhabited. The word is similar to *duthaich*, which means ancestral homeland, and has the same root, *du(th)*, which itself derives from an old Indo-European word meaning earth. Michael Newton, who traced this and other words of my heritage in his 2009 book, *Warriors of the Word*, quoted another source asserting that *duthchas* means not only ancestral land and traditions but even the "hereditary qualities of an individual."[1]

A sense of how intimate this affiliation was survives in the old Scottish tradition of a king's inauguration being traditionally called *banais-rige*, or "king-marriage." Becoming a king was a symbolic union with the goddess believed to be sovereign over that region. In the ritual, the king pledged her his troth, vowing to be true to her in all that this might mean. As for the implicit pledge around the *duthchas*, the clan chieftan was the official keeper of this responsibility, but according to Alasdair MacMhaoirn who teaches Gaelic and Highland Studies in a college on the Isle of Skye, it was shared by all and lived by all in everyday life.[2]

What intrigued me most about the *duthchas* was how these rights and responsibilities suggested an indivisible link between people and the land. The traditions and ways of relating both to one's neighbors and to the land were intricately interwoven together — a "heritage in the soil," as one account put it.[3] Was I risking overinterpretation if I thought that *duthchas* suggested even a living covenant with the land, I asked in a follow-up e-mail to Skye? Professor MacMhaoirn didn't think so. "I think you understand the idea," he wrote back.

Even when people became tenant farmers subject to rent, old ways of thinking continued and the king's law supported them, for a while. The Leases Act of 1449, for example, protected people "that labour the ground" in traditional commons, no matter who legally owned the land.[4] The tenancy was still considered a "trust unit," in the old *duthchas* tradition, not a commercial one.[5]

Moreover, even as the modern sense of land as owned property advanced and clan chiefs were given, or forced to take up, formal *feu charters* (see Chapter 8) to their traditional lands, the customary law of the *duthchas* still prevailed. According to an 1811 account by Anne Grant, cited in Newton's book, the chieftain "was not allow'd to part with territory [even] for the preservation of his life.... the habit of making all private considerations subservient to the good of the community" held.[6]

I don't want to read too much into a past that for people like my ancestors was recorded mostly in memories of repeated stories and proverbs, only fragments and faint echoes of which remain. Still, these notions of land occupancy as a trust rather than a commercial arrangement, and perhaps too a shared covenant with the Earth, go to the heart of what might be called the *ethos of the commons* and the common good. It's an ethos that I like to think could be revived if some of the practices that sustained it can be recovered. Just as life cannot be patented, the land and water of the Earth, which are equally alive, cannot be fully appropriated into patents of private property. This older truth can still prevail.

Duthchas is not a land claim as we've come to understand the word today. Or rather, what's claimed isn't land as property, but a lineage of connection and a responsibility toward a particular piece of land, as place, that's passed on from generation to generation. I recall not only that common means "together as one" or together in obligation, but that its opposite (that is, the opposite of *communis* being *immunis*) is being "not under obligation" or "exempt."[7] In other words, the ethos of the commons knit people together with their neighbors and with the land, plus the local fens, forest and bodies of water, with no one or nothing treated as exempt, nor as an externality. Inhabitants and habitat were one inseparable whole. All were neighbors, all belonged together, though this didn't rule out resentment and dissent. The point was that all were also bound together by mutual obligation and mutual self-interest, and reminded of this every day.

There was a place for individualism and self-interest, clearly, in the fact that every family had their own home and kailyard, their own allotted strip of the infield for growing oats and barley and their own cows and sheep, hens and ducks. But the selfishness of that self-interest was tempered by the network of interdependent relationships through which they did everything, in shares, and the shared knowledge on which they based their joint decision-making. This knowledge included the how of laboring the land and knowing the soil, collecting firewood from the forest and watching how the forest fared, excavating bog iron and peat from the fens, observing the waterfowl and knowing where and when to gather some of their eggs — and perhaps intoning some words of thanks while they did so. The bond was indivisible and sustained by daily practices of work, of learning and sharing knowledge, of tradition, story and song, proverb, ritual and prayer. All of this was embedded in the unfolding of life itself, the webwork of daily life.

Knowing the habitat through the dailiness of inhabiting it was important. So was the sense that the spirits of the ancestors inhabited it with you, living on at the site where their bodies were laid to rest. This is why ancestors' graves often marked boundaries, and anyone making claim to land as their ancestral home was expected to enter the land at this spot, with the idea that the spirits would recognize them and welcome them back, or not. It's probably also why people didn't say they came from a certain place. Instead, they said "*Buinidh mi do*", which means "I belong to" this place. As Newton wrote: "In Gaelic culture, people belong to places, rather than places belonging to people."[8]

This affiliation isn't that different, I'm sure, from how North America's tribal people saw and often still see themselves in relation to the land. As Canadian economic historian Irene Spry wrote in "The Tragedy of the Loss of the Commons in Western Canada," land was "the common property of everyone in the tribe or band. All might use this as the tribe or band decided, in accordance with their customs."[9] In *Common as Air*, Lewis Hyde wrote that historically the Native American "way of being human ... consisted of taking one's 'self' to be a common thing, and took the land held in common to be that self's material representation ... the place where it could exercise its rights of action and so have presence, standing, dignity."[10]

As I explored the remnants of fens and walked upland common pastures, sensing almost a spirit presence in the mist drifting down from the upper hill, I tried to imagine my ancestors here. I tried to imagine how they worked out the practical meaning of this deep connection through bylaws they discussed and adopted at regular common meetings, called *nabec* (meaning neighborliness) held at the local *public house* (pub), and through the selection of field officers trusted to keep watch and regulate things like access to the forest and infields for post-harvest gleaning to ensure that the common good prevailed. I tried to imagine too how they went about their work, with songs sung in rounds so that a shared cadence set the tone for coordinating action.

I imagined my ancestors' lives as a continuity of relationships, thick with knowledge and traditions, and fecund with feeling — no doubt some of it misery, frustration and the desire to flee or rebel at times. But still, running through it, like ley lines of telluric energy under the surface of the Earth[11], there would have been this feeling of connection, an identity inextricably linked to the land plus family and neighbors with whom my commoning ancestors worked the land. Their very identity was indivisible from the land that sustained their lives, and how well they came to know it. No wonder features of the topography were likened to body parts, even intimate ones like breast and penis. These people inhabited the land intimately and knew it that intimately as well. As I walked, feeling as though the spirits of my ancestors might be hovering somewhere in the mist descending from the hills, I began to understand why in Scotland someone with no ties to the land was called "a broken man."[12]

A sense of *duthchas* settled over me as I walked down from the hills above the Tay and Glen Lyon rivers, as I bent to wash my face in the stream that had probably burbled exactly that way in the days of my ancestors, flicking tiny drops of spray off the rocks into their faces too. It grew in me as I followed the curvature of the hill and came to a rocky outcrop with deep fissures between the jagged stones, and knew why my ancestors had brought goats to the shieling pasture as well as sheep. Because they would have known that goats are territorial and always choose rough, higher ground, effectively keeping the more lame-prone sheep away. And who knows — perhaps a particularly treacherous stretch of cliff and fissure carried a name that carried a story warning of such danger? I think of the spot on Baffin Island that the Inuit call *millurialik*, which means "throwing place." It marked the spot where native whale hunters traditionally threw boulders into an inlet to block beluga whales from escaping when the tide went out.[13]

This deep knowledge of interconnected relationships, people to animals and animals to land, is part of my heritage. It's a heritage of consciousness, and identity too, one that is connected to the land, even embedded in Creation.

Coming Home to the Sacred

I KNEW NOTHING ABOUT CELTIC CHRISTIANITY before I began this journey. But I started to pay attention when I learned that Dull, a mere stone's throw from Tullicro, had once been a major center of Celtic Christian learning, and that its scholarship formed the foundation of St. Andrew's University. Then I was given the key to the library in Castle Menzies, a great slab of an iron latchkey, and spent a morning leafing through old parish and tenancy records, plus a tome called *The Red & White Book of Menzies* where I read about a certain Saint David Menzies. He had been a monk in the Royal Monastery at Montrose, founded in the heyday of Celtic Christianity, then became a local cleric and died in 1449 at the age of 72. He was revered as a local saint for his piety and good works in the community and also for his habit of retiring to a spot in the hills, now known as the Rock of Weem. It's a spot where a spring bubbles out of the base of an overhanging cliff forming a cave at the time, "a cave wherein he exercised his devotions."[1] I knew immediately the spot being referred to, having found it on the path of a trail known as the Weem Woods walk, and having noticed a plaque set into the cliff above a spring-fed pool that read "Saint David's Well."

I packed my daypack with my usual supplies — water bottle and something good to eat — and set off in a slight mist of rain. The hill was steep, with many switchbacks and even some stairs set into the steepest inclines. But I was so eager to get to Saint David's Well that I almost ran. It felt like I was coming home to myself spiritually. I looked at the plaque, then at the pool of clear, cool water beneath it, fed by a moss- and watercress-lined stream that ran along the base of the cliff. I followed it back to its source, where the water flowed with the barest of sibilant sounds from a cleft in the dark, wet face of pure rock. All was quiet around me save for a bird in a bush close by and the sound of the water finding its way toward the stillness of the pool. I took my thermos out of my pack, dumped the contents off to the side, then tilted its mouth toward where the water emerged from the Earth. Then I lifted the thermos to my lips and drank.

"This do in remembrance of me" ran through me with all the force of a habit learned from growing up in a Presbyterian Church. Only suddenly what had symbolized the blood of Christ, the blood of atonement, had become the lifeblood of the Earth, which water surely is.

From what I have read of my earliest ancestors, the Picts were like many tribal people whose lives were and sometimes still are intimately entwined with the basic elements of life. They considered the whole Earth, their lifeworld, as sacred. Not only did they regard animals as kin; the MacDodrums of the Hebrides were nicknamed "the seal people" because they were said to be descended from seals.[2] An archaic female spirit called Cailleach appears in old oral tales as stopping hunters from killing too many deer. In a later story, she appears to a hunter in a traditional keening gesture of grief. She is understood to be lamenting the loss of the forest and the wilderness.[3] It reminds me of a legend a Déline elder, Morris Neyelle, told me about a lake called *Sahtu,* or Great Bear Lake, in Canada: that there's a heart beating in the middle of the lake, "the water heart."[4]

The Picts believed too that gods and goddesses existed in specific elements — such as the sun and the rain — and even resided in particular sites, such as caves and mountain tops, springs and wells, groves and special, sacred trees. Fish personified divine power, and salmon were revered as both wise and prophetic.

Still, the fourth-century Christian newcomers — called *peregrini* — introduced something wholly new: a God distinguishable from the living world and its elements, but not separate from them either. The message these pilgrims and Jesus movement messengers preached was of God embedded in Creation, including in human beings and the societies they created. As such, God was both of nature and of human society while at the same time more than the sum of both, and beyond anyone's power of reckoning. Trying to imagine the unimaginable, these early Christians described God as a great spirit, a sacred fire and energy pervading and animating everything from the wind in the trees, the sea on the shore and the spring waters bubbling out of the rocks, to the flowers and the grass and all living creatures. It imbued them too with a sense of mutual affinity, if not love, through which to weave their interdependent lives together. This notion of God as immanent in all creation, not transcendent and remote, was one of the most enduring features of Celtic Christianity.[5]

This Christianity as it was practiced by people like my ancestors is full of merged beliefs. Mary is often linked to Brigit, a pan-Celtic goddess associated with fertility, especially the fecundity of field crops and keeping them safe until harvest. Christ was sometimes referred to as a "sheltering branch" of the tree of life[6] or likened to a salmon or trout — and therefore, full of wisdom. One old Celtic Christian prayer that has survived refers to Christ as "the salmon of the well of mercy."[7] Colum Cille, who is thought to have founded the church at Dull, referred to Christ as "my Druid;"[8] Druid translates as "the man by the sacred oak who knew the truth."[9] By returning to places like the well or pool at the base of the cliff above Weem to pray and meditate, people like David Menzies kept alive a sense of the sacred embedded in the landscape. Perhaps too, he helped reinforce this among the people as they sang a sense of the sacred into their everyday lives. I discovered a remarkable anthology of Celtic hymns, prayers and incantations transcribed from the oral tradition by a retired government excise man, Alexander Carmichael, in the 1850s. It's called *Carmina Gadelica* and includes hymns and prayers for every imaginable daily event and task, including to kindle the hearth fire in the morning and to smoor or smother it at night to ensure some embers stay alive until morning. There are songs to accompany every kind of work these people did, sometimes alone but more often, together: weaving and waulking cloth; mowing the grain, binding it into sheaves and stooking these to dry for a few days before gathering them into the fermtoun barn for threshing and, in turn, grinding the grain, using a horse-powered quern or grindstone in the shared barnyard.

My favorite song is the one that women used when they sat down to milk the cows — perhaps because I too have milked cows by hand, though crudely and without much success:

> Bless, O God, my little cow,
> Bless, O God, my desire;
> Bless Thou my partnership
> And the milking of my hands, O God.
> Bless, O God, each teat,
> Bless, O God, each finger;
> Bless Thou each drop
> That goes into my pitcher, O God.

"After this prayer," Carmichael's notes continued, "the woman sings songs and croons, lilts and lullabies to cow after cow til all are milked. The secular songs and the religious songs of the people are mixed and mingled, song and hymn alternating in unison with the movements of the hands and the idiosyncrasies of the milker."

He continued: "Nor is it less interesting to observe the manner in which the cows themselves differentiate between the airs sung to them, giving their milk freely with some songs and withholding it with others. Occasionally a cow will withhold her milk til her own favourite lilt is sung to her. The intelligence of these Highland cows is instructive and striking to the student of nature. These differences are well known to the observant people themselves, who discuss them and discriminate between certain traits in the nature and character of their cows and horses and other animals."[10]

Right relations, I thought, as I returned to Tullicro, my thermos full of water from the spring. I stood in the spot at the east end of the shuttered and padlocked crux cottage where the cow byre used to be, the animals sheltered under the same longhouse roof as the humans, and I tried to imagine myself sitting down here to milk a cow. I thought of the words I might have sung every morning and evening, the cadences settling the cow and me into shared rhythm, the cow ready to give her milk, my hands ready to receive it. Prayer would have slipped like a glove over each finger, enveloping me, the cow and our "partnership," the words invoking a blessing on my work-roughened hands as I prepared for the task at hand.

As I imagined this, I caught a glimpse, a hint of what it might have been like to be immersed in a spirit world that is entwined with the most basic material elements of everyday life, survival and well-being. It didn't matter whether God could be proved to exist or not, far off in some remote heaven or, in fact, present in the cows and teats and fingers going about tasks like milking. What mattered were the faith practices, the dailyness of them, the pervasiveness of them. What mattered was acting from that place of grounded faith, working the energy flows of attuned connection. It was a spirit habitat as real as the soil in the yard outside, making not just the waters of a spring and the wilds of the hills but even the gravelly ground of the kailyard sacred. A habitat of close interrelationship and mutual attunement.

It's not surprising to me then to find that for my ancestors, sin was associated with letting slip the practices that sustained this sense of attunement. J. Philip Newell, a scholar and former warden of Iona Abbey, quoted ninth-century Celtic Christian teacher, John Scotus Eriugena, as likening sin to "leprosy of the soul," a reference to a distinguishing physiological characteristic of that disease, which is loss of sensitivity in the skin.[11] It's around this that I imagine the possible role of another hallmark of Celtic Christianity: the *anam cara* or soul friend, an institution in which one honed sensitivity to others and an affinity for sacred connection. Soul friends weren't exalted or particularly specialized people in the community, I've learned. They were ordinary people, in the same ways that the original apostles and friends of Jesus were ordinary people. They were meant to be friends to each other, equals who were at the same time devoted to calling out the best in each other, bending and shaping self and self-interest toward right relations, community and the common good. *Credit*, in those days and in that society, was a quality of character, specifically one's reliability as a good neighbor, one who could be counted upon to share, to show up in a crisis, to do a share of work, not a type of financing. (Interestingly too, some commons jurisdictions actually fined people for such offences as refusing to share the use of a cart.)[12]

In *Celtic Christian Spirituality*, Mary C. Earle wrote that "a soul friend is a person who will allow you to tell the whole truth of yourself, and encourage you to seek healing and restoration." It is a relationship of "mutual disclosure," she said, requiring that each be "humble enough to seek correction and guidance from a friendly presence." There's also enormous faith: it was understood at the time that in learning to live in right relations with Creation, one moved closer to fulfilling the divine. The potential for this and the potential to live at one with Creation are implanted in our humanity, according to early Christian thought, though guidance and discipline are required to cultivate it. A soul friend, Earle wrote, provided that guidance and encouragement, kindling "the divine fire within the soul," much like Jesus did, serving as a soul friend to his friends, the disciples.[13]

First Nations communities in North America have origin stories that impart the principles of community and the common good, and I've learned a lot about this through Richard Atleo and his books of native spiritual philosophy called *Tsawalk: A Nuu-chh-nulth Worldview*, plus its sequel, *Principles of Tsawalk: An Indigenous Approach to Global Crisis*. Some stories narrate simply the connection between people and the earth and sky, while others impart key teachings on how to maintain balance and harmony. Together, they teach what Atleo describes as the four constitutional principles of life: recognition, consent, respect — including "sacred respect," holding all Creation in reverence — and continuity. In Atleo's view, practising this philosophy starts with recognition because that involves the opening up of the self to see "another as important, to see value in the other," and the necessary humility that this involves.[14]

What similar stories my ancestors might have shared seem to have been lost and forgotten. However, there are proverbs. Scottish lore is full of proverbs, which travel well in the oral tradition and pack a lot of wisdom. I found a few in Michael Newton's book, including:

+ A person by himself is not a person.
+ Two things should not be empty: the stomach of the old and the hand of the child
+ Despite the shape of the peat, you can find a place in the stack for it.[15]

I can imagine these proverbs being turned over and over in conversation between two soul friends sitting by the peat fire on a winter's afternoon, the glow from the slow-burning turf ruddy in their faces. A lot of the proverbs have to do with doing the right thing. For example, "Wrong will not rest, nor will ill-deed stand" and "A lie will not live for long." Others speak more to the need to develop one's character, and the capacity to discern what the right thing is amidst the complexities and contradictions of daily life. It's a quality known in Gaelic as *naire*, the capacity to know what is wrong and right. One proverb maintains that the person who's lost his or her *naire* has lost everything.[16]

It strikes me that a soul friendship dialogue might have been a kind of commoning on a spirit level, nurturing a sense of the self and its dwelling place in the world that might parallel the commoning practiced in daily tasks and self-governing common decision-making. Perhaps soul friendship was the spiritual equivalent of keeping the field "in good heart," only at this level more by cultivating an attunement to others and the living habitat and with it, a commitment to the common good, the shared welfare or well-being of all. In other words, becoming an *implicated participant* (see Glossary).

I turned and gazed out across the sheep pasture toward the mark stone that had become my thinking place. It might be simply a wishful leap of my imagination, but I think I'm onto something here in making this link between the anam cara and the common good. It's through relationships, and especially, I think, intentional relationships such as the anam cara, the elder and the mentor that the common good can begin to mean something. It's through relationships and community that you common your humanity and share your existence with others. It's through relationships that your identity extends outward, becomes vested in something larger than your solitary self. Speaking from the ancestral ways he names himself as having been born into, Richard Atleo describes it as a "macro" or "group" stream of perception of the self coexisting with a "micro" or "individual" self-perception.[17] I recall something Irene Spry wrote about the Cree: "The great satisfaction of the strong, the clever, the wise and the skilled was that they could contribute to the well-being of the whole community. Self-respect and social esteem were won by ability and readiness to share generously with others, by adding to the general welfare of the community. There were dandies and self-seeking people, of course, but they were tolerated, not admired."[18]

Canada's First Nations brought a common-good ethos to their earliest encounters with newcomers from France and England. In his 2008 book *A Fair Country*, John Ralston Saul noted that when the Cree were negotiating with British newcomers in what is now the Canadian Prairies, they did so on the basis of *Witaskewin*, which Saul described as "an idea of carefully negotiated and continually renegotiated peaceful co-existence." In turn, Saul wrote, peaceful coexistence is based on the related concept of sharing, which includes sharing space. This, in turn, is "dependent upon *Wahakohtoin*," which means "relationships that work because they follow a complex, unwritten code of ethics." If these practices, these protocols and this code of ethics are pursued with integrity, the end result is what the Cree call *Miyo-wicehtowin* — "good, healthy, happy, respectful relationships."[19]

Saul went on to identify this common-good ethos in some of the earliest documents naming the new country called Canada and what it stood for. He argued that James Murray, Guy Carleton, Robert Baldwin and Louis-Hippolyte LaFontaine tacitly extended these aboriginal concepts in their own elaborations of governance, as they emphasized public peace, welfare, *bien-etre* (well-being) and good government in such early documents as the 1701 Great Peace of Montreal, the 1764 Niagara Peace, the Royal Proclamation of 1763, the Constitutions of 1791 and of 1840. In an erudite aside, Saul noted that when Guy Carleton translated the Quebec Act into French, welfare became *bonheur* and *le bonheur futur*. Thus, Saul wrote, "*welfare* meant *happiness* in the eighteenth-century sense. That sense was the fulfillment of the self within the shared well-being of society."[20]

Can we recover this implicated sense of connection both to Creation and the common good? And how was it lost in the first place? From what I've learned, this consciousness didn't simply die away under the progressive influence of modernity. The ethos was eroded as the practices that sustained it as a living ethos were discredited or overruled, and as *duthchas*' traditional ties to the land were dismissed as "a legal nonsense."[21]

The Tragedy of the Commons Revisited

THE TRAGEDY OF THE LOSS OF THE COMMONS IS MANY THINGS. Most famously, though, it is a story that has been accepted as gospel, yet for which no empirical evidence was ever offered. As Susan Buck wrote in "No Tragedy on the Commons," it was a Tonypandy, a fiction that is allowed to persist even by those people who know better.[1] According to a much-quoted 1968 essay by environmentalist Garret Hardin titled "The tragedy of the Commons," the commons of England and Scotland disappeared because they were unsustainable, given the utilitarian logic of the day. According to this, every "rational herdsman" as Hardin put it, would want to maximize his individual profit, and so would send one too many sheep to the common pastureland. The inevitable too many sheep would overgraze the pasture, would exceed its carrying capacity and would drive the land into a desert-like state of barrenness. "Freedom in a common brings ruin to all," Hardin wrote with finality.[2]

Hardin didn't base this conclusion on a careful historical examination of various self-governing commons and stinting regulations through which local inhabitants limited the number of sheep and cows sent to the common pasture, based on a logic of the common good. He based his conclusion on a pamphlet written in 1832 by an amateur mathematician, William Forster Lloyd, first made public as a lecture Lloyd gave at Oxford University. Lloyd cited no common knowledge, and quoted no commoners in making his claim that this was how people living on the commons thought and acted. Like others associated with the Improvement Movement, Lloyd relied on new, more abstract forms of knowledge, knowledge practices associated with modern science and utilitarian thinking. He simply assumed that everyone thought in these rational, self-serving terms. He also cloaked his assumption behind numbers, extrapolations from census records on numbers of people and animals.[3] Like other self-styled progressives of his time, he chose the seeming objectivity of data and mathematical projections — the computer modeling of his day — over direct observation and stories of people's actual experience.

If Lloyd had descended from his Oxford podium, if he'd taken the newfangled steam train north to Edinburgh and a stagecoach north from there to Aberfeldy and walked across the bridge to Tullicro, if he'd arrived in May, around the time called Beltane on the old pagan calendar and had opened his ears to the voices all around him, he would have witnessed the annual flitting to the upland common pasture, the shieling. The *flitting*, as it was called, was a major annual pilgrimage, with most of the fermtoun emptying out, partly as a conservation measure, to let the local pastures rest and revive. In the first of two stages, young men and older boys drove the horses and oxen to the shieling as soon as spring field work was done in late April, and made basic repairs to the bothies and folds. Older men, women and children followed, in the "big flitting" in May, bringing spinning tools and hand looms for working cloth, cheese frames for pressing the cheeses that would be made at the shieling during the summer, plus spades for digging peats, some shoots and potato cuttings for a kailyard fashioned from a stack of fresh peats and perhaps too some snares for rabbits and a bodron or two to beat out the rhythm for telling the old stories and singing the old songs — often hybrids of pagan and Christian lyrics.

Although the animals were herded to and pastured on the shieling common all together, the numbers that could be sent from each family were carefully allotted, according to stints or limits set out by the field officers. The stinting rate, in turn, was based on observations from the previous years shared not just by field officers but by everyone at seasonal meetings of the fermtoun common. And so, with the authority of the entire common behind them, the young people went out from the fermtoun's walls, driving the animals along single-track dirt roads, using loans or driftways (common rights-of-way through others' lands) as they headed into the waste lands of the higher hills. Special field officers called *herds* kept the animals on track, while other field officers, called *drifters*, kept count of them, ensuring that no one had snuck in an extra sheep above their designated share. There were consequences in the event that someone pulled a fast one. The *pinfold* was a pound where errant animals were kept, either because they'd exceeded the stinting rate or, close to home, had strayed into the infield where wheat, oats and barley were grown. *Pounders* or *poindlers* were the equivalent of local constables responsible for ensuring that stints were honored, and taking corrective action if they weren't.[4] Fines levied for these and other infractions of the local bylaws went into a Common Good fund for purchasing, for example, breeding bulls.[5]

All of this self-organization and self-governance was local, recognized as *lex loci* which, while simply local custom or *praxis loci*, had legal effect.[6] It was vested in the local oral culture and part of a local social and economic order of which the market was an adjunct and regulated according to the needs of the community. Commoning was a particular way of weaving the threads of daily life, the how of things with the why to give meaning and a sense of what's real and relevant, and it lasted for centuries, with the blessing of church and state including the Tudor kings and the early Stuarts.

By the 17th century, however, the allegiance of church and state was shifting. A new modern sensibility was emerging, associated with Protestantism, Utilitarian philosophy and with it, notions of progress and individual self-improvement. The Agricultural Revolution, the first of three modern technological revolutions (the others being the industrial and, most recently, the digital), was afoot. A new form of society, called the nation-state was also emerging and at its core, a new understanding of economy, as commercial, centered in a market ruled by supply and demand, not the relations of local life as these were informed by necessity.[7] This new society was served by new, faster forms of transportation, which drew in surpluses from more commercial farms and expanded the scale of commerce from regional and national markets to a burgeoning British empire.

The changes involved were myriad and complex. One of the most fascinating was how the means of ordering and naming reality changed, and in turn changed the perception of reality itself. Maps are one example. Premodern maps were hand-drawn pictures, with stylized renderings of hills and streams, trees and buildings all faithful to what they looked like in real life, and how life was lived there day to day. Modern maps, however, were representations of spatial abstractions, with these abstractions derived from surveys of the land, not the land itself. The resultant new maps used a grid of latitude and longitude lines to designate the boundaries of land now as property, no longer habitat. This standard measure also allowed large-scale maps to be produced that could be used for reference when enclosure petitions were brought to parliament. These were petitions to enclose various tracts of commons, to convert the land to sheep walks or some other commercial farming venture. Surveying, with its signature measuring chain, was crucial in this new representation of land as measured abstraction. Until surveying introduced a grid and progressive numbers to the measuring of space, the measure of land was understood through how people worked it. An acre, for example, was simply how much ground could be ploughed in a day. In other words, the reality of "an acre" was embedded in people's direct relations with and experience of the land. Now it was disembedded, and a new reality embedded in a portable, survey-based map. As a 1617 surveyor's handbook put it, the purpose and value of surveying was: "to reduce all sorts of grounds into a square for the better measuring of it."[8]

And so, as Robert A. Dodgshon wrote in "Everyday Structures, Rhythms and Spaces of the Scottish Countryside," "A landscape that had hardly known a straight line, in which natural ecology always had the upper hand in shaping farm layout, was now covered with the un-compromisingly regular shapes and lines of the surveyor."[9]

Changes in the law were another example of this curious shift. In the early 17th century pioneering jurist, Edward Coke (later, Sir Edward Coke) took it upon himself to review the varied local laws of the land and systematize them into one national set of standard prec-edents, called English Common Law. As Nicholas Blomley put it in *Law, Space and the Geographies of Power*, "the 'geographies' of order" shifted during this period, from being immersed and embedded in the land to being embedded in documents: surveys, maps, legal texts and deeds of property. As with maps, the new law severed justice and its accountability from local contexts. What had been a dialogue couched in local relationships and long-standing customs and precedents for interpreting what was right became formal arguments accountable to remote standards and authorities. Meanwhile, these new geographies of order became the new medium for the ordering of reality, both on the ground and in people's heads.[10] What had been a right to com-mon (to farm or pasture livestock) as an inhabitant of a place since time immemorial was slowly worn down into a privilege and finally taken away.[11] The new ordering of knowledge through modern science played its part as well, as Rene Descartes famously drew a line separat-ing mind from matter (and from body), and Francis Bacon famously advocated using the new mechanical arts to subdue nature, to shape her as on an anvil.[12]

People like William Forster Lloyd were part of this new realm of knowing. They were among a new elite of knowledge producers for whom the test of knowledge was less in actual experience and more in official texts featuring theoretical formulations and statistics. Arthur Young was another of the self-styled agricultural "improvers" of the day, proselytizing about the vast increases in yield per acre to be had after enclosing fields and applying modern farming techniques. At least one historian has questioned the accuracy of his numbers; still, his methods and his medium were considered authoritative.[13] And his message was useful to the other agenda behind the clearances that enclosing land brought on: making people dependent on jobs and wages in the emerging industrial economy. As a Shropshire resident put it in a submission to the Board of Agriculture in 1794: "The use of common land by laborers operates upon the mind as a sort of independence … [Whereas after enclosure,] the labourers will work every day in the year, their children will be put out to labour early, [resulting in] the subordination of the lower ranks of society which in the present times is so much wanted."[14] Similarly, Walter Blith, an agricultural theorist and proponent of enclosures argued that commons were a moral evil encouraging residents in "all manner of idleness and mischief."[15] Another commentator, John Bellers, described the Commons as "a hindrance to industry and … Nurseries of Idleness and Insolence."[16]

And so the narrative continued. What had been decried as greed under the old social order was now called thrift. Commoners like my ancestors were disparaged for being illiterate and therefore ignorant, even willfully backward and lazy.

I sat on the mark stone on the edge of what is now a sheep pasture near my bothy, hugging my knees and taking this in. It was my first inkling of what it feels like to be a colonized person, the realities of my family's history distorted or disappeared. I've worked and identified with the side of privilege for so long I had only understood it intellectually until that moment.

Feudal Land Charters and Private Property

T HE SEEDS OF TREATING LAND AS PROPERTY WERE LAID EARLY in the British Isles, at the time of the Norman Conquest. Feudal culture means many things but at its heart was a feu charter of land. This was introduced to England by the Normans who formalized their control over the conquered territory by sharing that control through land charters, called feu charters, given first to their own and, later, Anglo-Norman barons; though retaining control over any minerals under the ground for the crown. The lords and barons, in turn, pledged loyalty to the king, plus ongoing dues and pledges of food from the land and able-bodied men to serve as soldiers when the need for an army arose.

Scotland wasn't originally included in this feudal system that replaced an *allodial* understanding of land (with no remote authority conferring rights of occupation) with state control — that is, *nulle terre sans seigneur* (no land without its superior).[1] But starting in 1124, King David I used feu charters to claim overarching control over this northern domain, drawing on a pool of Norman or Anglo-Norman nobles, including Robert du Brus (Robert the Bruce), to be his feudal agents. Under these charters, customary claims to live on and labor the land were redefined as "by tolerance"[2] under *baile* tenancies subject to rent, which for centuries took an in-kind form as so many "stones" of cheese, bales of wool, bushels of grain and lambs for slaughter.³ There were still commons, but the old way of understanding the land as inseparable from the people inhabiting it as they always had was now officially considered legal nonsense.

By 1500 in Scotland, many traditional clan chiefs had applied for and received feu charters. But many had not, and some historians think this was because to do so would have violated the bond of connection between the chief, the people and the land associated with the *duthchas*. In 1597, an Act was passed requiring all clan chiefs to produce proof of their title to the soil where their people lived, in the form of a feu charter, or lose the land. But still there was resistance. In 1608, Scotland's leading Highland chiefs were kidnapped by the king and imprisoned, in three separate castles in Lowland, Scotland, for 10 months. They were freed only when they agreed to sign a covenant promising to suppress the old clan-based cultural practices and also to send their eldest sons away to private schools in England for their education, to be better assimilated into the emergent more urban and class-based society.⁴ These residential schools did their work well, cultivating in a new Scottish aristocracy a taste for the good life and the necessary dependency on wealth and its generation that this required.⁵

Meanwhile, John Locke, considered the father of modern economics for his pioneering treatises published in the late 1690s, linked this individualized form of landholding to utilitarian gain with his theorizing about something called property. Originally, *property* had a more qualitative meaning. It was a characteristic, a claim to preference or a use-right to something.⁶ People talked about having a right of common, associated with a field or a pasture. This meant they had a right to make use of that field to grow something, or of that pasture to graze or fatten some livestock. Locke not only ignored the collective, cooperative nature of the common. He saw this as a negative not a positive thing because the common belonged to no individual. Focusing on the individual, he argued that people created "property" through the work of their hands improving the land of the common. As E.P. Thompson put it in *Customs in Common*, "Locke took as a paradigm of the origin of property the mixing of labour (which was man's only original 'prop-erty', in himself and in his own hands) with the common:' Whatsoever, then, he removes out of the state that nature hath provided and left it in, he hath mixed his labour with ... and thereby makes it his proper-ty,'"he quoted Locke as having argued.7

The argument was embraced by champions of agricultural improve-ment. Leaving land in a state of"unimproved" commons was increasingly depicted, in pamphlets and the popular press, as "economically un-sound," "a moral evil" and, to John Locke, primitive. Locke described the North American Indian as "still a tenant in common ... knowing no enclosure." But the Indians were poor as a result, he maintained, "for want of improving [the land] through labour."8

Other thinkers built on this idea. Sir. William Blackstone argued that the law (Coke's modern law of the land of England) should recog-nize property rights as exclusive. As E.P. Thompson wrote in *Customs in Common*: "What was happening, from the time of Coke to that of Blackstone, was a hardening and concretion of the notion of property in land, and a re-ification of usages into properties which could be rented, sold or willed."9 Thompson went on to note that Adam Smith, in his 1776 *Wealth of Nations*, argued that the state and the courts should champion people's claims to private property "which is acquired by the labour of many years, or perhaps of many successive generations..."10

Still, the right of common retained some of its old meaning, if not as a right of collective agency, at least as an individual's or family's claim to use what common land was still available. And people struggled to guard that claim — pasturing a cow here, growing a small strip of oats there or collecting peat in the uplands — even while they sold their capacity to labor the land now as weavers, carpenters, wheelrights or as hired hands in the industrial-scale factories in nearby towns and cities or on the estates of increasingly money-minded local lairds. The old order was tenacious, however. Even if the integrity of self-governing fermtouns was gone and the enforceability of local stinting regulations too, remnants of the commons and its traditions persisted. It took the Clearances to bring them to an end.

9

The Real Tragedy of the Loss of the Commons

THE REAL TRAGEDY OF THE LOSS OF THE COMMONS is that phrases like "barren as a common" weren't inevitable. They were brought into being. The degradation and loss of the commons was made to happen. It was contrived from laws and conceptions of land as property to be improved by human labor. These concepts were part of a new social order that was portrayed in the new print media of the day as the irresistible march of progress, with anyone resisting it disparaged as backward or hopelessly romantic. Such people were clinging to a past that was no longer tenable, in the eyes of the Improvers and their ways of both ordering and rendering what was real and realistic.

In fact, the self-governing commons was and still is a viable social and economic institution. Elinor Ostrom was awarded the Nobel Prize in Economics in 2009 for her landmark work rebutting the "tragedy of the commons" argument. Through careful research on historical and present-day self-governing commons, she showed that commoners have in the past and still do tackle the age-old problem of the selfish free rider. It's addressed through practices of stinting, of overseeing this through transparent reporting and through enforcement and real consequences for the rule breakers, plus by building up mutual trust and a shared sense of the common good through relationship building and working together over time.[1]

Nevertheless, in Scotland at the time of the Clearances, petitions to enclose common lands were approved by the hundreds and thousands.[2] Between these and what was called *rack renting*, as annual rents were raised by as much as 50% a year,[3] the commons where my people had lived for centuries were lost. Fences were put up to keep the common people off the land, gamekeepers assigned to keep them from poaching or foraging for firewood there, and they were evicted from the fermtouns or townships where they'd lived as extended families and clan kin for centuries. Sometimes this was by force, with soldiers sent north across General Wade's stone bridge to torch the thatch of the cottages and smash the chimney stacks as insurance against attempts at repossession. I walked through one such abandoned ruins of a fermtoun, not far from Tullicro. Trees now grow where women might have milked the cows or men tended to the querning of the grain. As I stood on what would have been a well-travelled path among the broken houses and byres, I could almost feel the erasure of human presence among the tumbled-down stones.

For me this is the real tragedy: the loss itself, the enormity of it. My forbears and their neighbors didn't just lose their together-as-one connection to the land. They lost all that these ties meant to them economically, politically, socially, culturally and even spiritually. They lost ways of working the land and working things out together. They lost ways of knowing the land directly, intimately through the soles of their feet, the tone of their muscled arms and hands, ways extended into the crafts that brought hand knowledge together with head knowledge in the spinning, carding and weaving of wool, in the threshing of grain, the making of cheese and ale, the shaping of plough boards and the tilling of fields. They lost ways of knowing the animals too, wild and domestic, and how they moved from woodland to water and claimed certain spots conducive to begetting. As well, they lost ways of sharing this experience, this knowing as *common knowledge*, with that knowledge both informing and supporting the authority of local decision-making.

They lost ways of celebrating life and honoring the stories buried in the names of springs and pools, mountain peaks and knobby bits of rocky outcrop.

Together, these ways added up to a whole identity, with lines of affiliation and identification extending from the individual self to others, to animals and birds and through the fabric of the land itself in all its varying features. All of it was a meshwork of cohabitation and well-being, including economic well-being and livelihood, with clearly defined rights supporting it: *piscary* being the right to fish, *turbury* being the right to cut peat or turf for fuel, *common of estover* being the right to take wood from the forest or waste land to repair gates or farm equipment such as plough boards. It was a way of life and even a way of being human that is sometimes identified as traditional and indigenous — "indigenous in the sense that they believe they belong to the space they occupy," according to John Mohawk, in *Renewing the Earth: The Promise of Social Ecology*.[4]

I wouldn't call my great, great grandparents who emigrated to Upper Canada in the ebbing of the Clearances "indigenous." Still, I think it's likely that something of that sensibility persisted in the commoning traditions they practiced in the 18th and early 19th century and in the commoning ethos that informed them. In what they did and how they did it, they still had the capacity to see and identify themselves as intricately connected with each other and the land. They were immersed in a shared agency that included both the local community and the commons habitat in which the community, in turn, was embedded. With the Clearances, they were uprooted, disconnected and displaced both from the land in which their lives had been so intimately involved and this collective agency, this power and capacity for local, ecological self-governance.

I got up from the table in the main front room of the bothy and fetched my research notes from my bag. Phrases jumped out at me now: the "close, nucleated villages" of the commons era;[5] the "miniature parliament" of the "self-governing village community,"[6] but also the distinctiveness of this "native system of governance."[7] It was embedded in daily life, in "a tangled skein of interpersonal connection" with the "'warp of self-preservation ... interwoven with the weft of neighbour-liness.'"[8] I began to grasp the significance of the commons being run not by law as much as by custom, "operative custom" which was "the outcome of cumulative adjustment.... or, in Tawney's striking phrase, 'a sort of great collective bargain'"[9] that was, moreover, ongoing. It was subject to ongoing negotiation and also to ongoing argument, as people "'threshed out'" conflicting goals and values against different readings of local reality.[10] Clearly, commoning carried the normal flaws and imperfections of any social institution. Still, it was a viable model of governance, what could be called a socio-ecological model. It was governance as and through relationships, human to human and human to land, and it didn't just fade away in the natural course of evolution. It was dismantled, almost deliberately.

I got up from the table and walked outside. I was aware of the stillness and silence of this former fermtoun as I hadn't been aware of it before. I was aware of it as absence. Absence of people and absence of voices talking, calling out instruction and correction, singing and chanting over shared work in the barnyard. I imagined these voices now as an aural net of connection, spun fresh daily, changing color and tone and content with the unfolding of the seasons, weaving the singers into a shared presence that was ongoing. And it extended outward, casting invisible threads as people walked the land, journeyed to and from the shieling or to clan gatherings, chanting the names of every cleft in the hill, every ridge and waterfall, knowing the stories behind each name, hearing them repeated as they went along their way. I imagine it as akin to the singing of traditional songlines by the Aboriginals of Australia. In their singing or the storytelling, the Highland people wove themselves anew into the landscape and affirmed their lineage, their storied and *duthchas* connection to the land. This too was lost with the Clearances. As Canadian poet and essayist Mark Abley wrote in *Spoken Here: Travels among Threatened Languages*, "without the stories, the land turns into real estate."[11]

On my last day in Scotland. I went to my mark stone thinking place, taking my daypack as a cushion. I sat there watching the clouds drifting past me down the valley, shape shifting as they went. I looked out across the hills upon hills in the distance, knowing that in Perthshire alone there are 20 different names for hills and peaks, each one speaking to a particular distinction of geomorphology. Not knowing either their names or the Gaelic that would communicate their storied meaning to me, all these are lost to me, like ancestors I never knew.

As I stared across the valley, I found myself recalling a comment made to describe the Indigenous peoples of what became the United States being cleared off their land in the 1880s. The reference was to the effect of the *Dawes Act* which parceled what had been shared tribal land into scattered individualized lots of private property, which most Native people couldn't relate to nor afford to keep. The effect of this displacement was devastating. It "plucked the Indian like a bird," the unknown commentator said.[12]

Tears welled up in my eyes as I recalled that telling phrase, here in the silence of this place where my ancestors commoned with each other and with the land. The comment sums up the tragedy of the loss of the commons wherever it has occurred or continues to occur: people stripped of their capacity to live in direct relations with the land, to know what they know in part out of that relationship and to come together as functioning, contributing, participating parts of a local community that is both social and natural habitat. My ancestors too were plucked of their traditional habitat and ways of being within it, then left to somehow live.

Part II

Reclaiming the Commons as Practices

From Premodern Past to Digital Present

I't's untrue to say that the Enclosure Movement and the Clearances have been going on ever since. Still, it's a thought I find myself playing with as I pack my bags, load them into my rental car and drive toward the airport in Glasgow. More and more life activities have been drawn into the orbit of the market economy, commoditized into goods and services. There is less focus on making hay, making bread, making a meal and making clothes for what these mean to people involved in the here and now of life. Instead, our focus is more on making money, and doing all these things in the most efficient way possible to make a profit, and to invest this to make more money still.

Over my lifetime, I have witnessed the ongoing enclosure of the commons. In Uganda and other parts of rural Africa long-standing customary use rights to some of the last remaining common lands on Earth are being ignored and the land turned over to foreign agribusiness with nothing seeming to stop the displacement of people who have always lived there, though the NGO Friends of the Earth International has been trying. Water as a commons is being undermined in a range of ways, from the outright privatization of water resources (in India and Ethiopia) to massive hydro-electric dams (on the Mekong River) or equally massive extraction of groundwater for irrigation and for the burgeoning bottled-water market.[1]

In my writing and conference speaking, I have also borne witness to what could be described as the ongoing dynamic of both enclosure and clearance. This happened in the 20th century through automation and the restructuring of national and multinational economies into one digitally integrated global economy. People were dislocated from communities and dispossessed both of their knowledge and of their capacity for collegial self-governance. There was public debate around this wave of technological change, but this debate proceeded much like the one that accompanied the first one, associated with the Agricultural Revolution and its ethos of "improvement." It was not framed broadly as between the moral and philosophical claims of two different conceptions of economy, but more narrowly around how the shift to a globally competitive corporate economy could best be accomplished, with minimal adjustment pain. The conversations I took part in focused on jobs and re-skilling.

I resisted this narrow frame, trying to focus on deeper losses and dislocations. I'd spent a night shift in a highly automated car factory learning about the loss of shop-floor community and shared, embodied knowledge from the men and a few women who were now mostly tending robots and working in isolation from each other. I'd travelled to Midland, Ontario and Ste. Agathe, Quebec when Bell Canada shut down rural telephone exchanges, amalgamating its largely automated call switching into a few centralized call centers. I sought out and got together with affected women in these rural communities because I wanted to hear their stories, and why they disliked the company's offer of retraining for work in the nearest call center. It wasn't just the distance of the commute or the outright relocation of family. For them, the local telephone exchange was inextricably embedded in the community. That is, they ran the local exchange as a community information center, providing Bell telephone services but also fielding calls from people wanting to know the time or the score in the high school hockey tournament. The women wished to continue this, using automated equipment located locally. But this option, this path of technological development that would simultaneously have been community development, was not even considered. Nor was there even a place for discussing it at the official conferences I attended. The agenda was entirely focused on utilitarian issues: helping people adjust to job losses plus retraining requirements for the new digital economy, with the need to be competitive remaining paramount. At the time, I felt frustrated and personally inadequate as I buckled down and learned to do what I was told to do if I wanted to be taken seriously: produce numbers, big numbers through computer modeling, on projected job losses. Now I see a larger historical frame: the displacement of any language or even a common sense of what's real and relevant, other than what's good for the global economy. I see too the inadequacy of mainstream public debates, not just about the social environment but nature's environment too, as part of these deeper losses.

The tragedy William Forster Lloyd calculated in 1832 might now in fact be coming true because so much of the Earth is owned and controlled by people whose choices are almost entirely governed by rational utilitarian thinking, with corporate self-interest trumping what's good for the community and the land. Equally, the residue of public-interest, common-good thinking associated with public policy, which used to balance self-interest, has been stripped away through decades of deregulation and public-sector cutbacks. What checks are left are little more than window dressing: social and environmental impact assessments mitigate disaster at best.

People's thinking has also become so weighted by what's cheap, fast, self-serving, cost-effective and convenient that concepts like social justice and the common good elicit little more than tax-deductible donations. It's as though we're all enclosed in essentially one way of thinking, one way of doing things and even one way of imagining what's real and doable. Even if it's possible to think along other lines, it's difficult to sustain meaningful collective action along them. Climate change and environmental degradation — social as well as natural — seem to be bearing down on us with the unstoppable force of tragedy.

In *The Great Transformation*, Karl Polanyi detailed the shift from a habitat-centered to a market-centered society, from an economy regulated by the social relations of community and ecological relations with the land to one regulated by the transactional relations of the market. The effect, he wrote, involved "no less a transformation than that of the natural and human substance of society into commodities," and "the running of society as an adjunct to the market." The resultant "dislocation," he concluded, "must disjoint man's relationships and threaten his natural habitat with annihilation."[2]

I lean my head against the plastic window frame of the plane I'm on high above the Atlantic Ocean. I'm tired, yet am also amazed at how far I have travelled in time and memory. I have walked the land with which my ancestors lived in direct relations. They knew it intimately, and how they worked, governed and sustained that land reflected what they knew. I have let the meaning of their work, decision-making and cultural practices permeate my being. I have opened myself to an understanding of Self as embedded in Habitat, in a network of relationships with other cohabitants and even, culturally and spiritually, as immersed in Creation. I have come to understand the loss of the commons as something that has cut deeply through time and space.

As I gaze out the plane window, at the vastness of open ocean unscrolling far beneath me, I realize too that in choosing to remember and to reconnect with my heritage on the commons, I have crossed a threshold of perception. I have discovered another path, another way of being in the world. It was cut off, abandoned and left to grow over; yet I have brought it back to life at least in my heart and imagination. I recognize it now as a possible path of reconnection, a place to stand in confronting the crises and impasse of our times.

It might be too late. But it might not, if a place to stand outside modern economistic thinking can be found. There might be some hope if something of the practices necessary both to forge an alternative path and credit it as real can be revived. The legacy of the self-governing commons, which is shared by many newcomers to North America from Britain, Europe and elsewhere too, offers such an alternative. This path is locally responsible, community-based and embedded in the land and local environment, much as traditional Indigenous cultures still are. As Elinor Ostrom wrote in her Nobel-prize winning work, the commons is an alternative to the prevailing choices in organizing society (through remote market control or remote state control).[3] It's also a pattern that is closely modeled after nature. As postmodern scientists associated with Chaos Theory, Systems Theory and Quantum Physics have discovered, in nature everything is one.[4] Everything is interrelated and interconnected in an ongoing dialogue of self-organizing co-creation and evolution. This new understanding simultaneously supports traditional knowledge systems and debunks the modern worldview associated with Isaac Newton, Rene Descartes and Francis Bacon. In this view, nature was inert matter subject to external laws and should be treated that way. The view conveniently dovetailed with the prevailing Christian worldview — that humans should have dominion over nature — an idea still central to contemporary conservative ideology, certainly in North America.

If there is a Great Turning, a shift in the collective unconscious, going on these days, it is a movement away from this model of reality, premised on external control and direction, toward another model on new and simultaneously ancient lines. In *Coming Back to Life*, Buddhist philosopher and teacher Joanna Macy (who coined the "Great Turning" phrase) described the shift as both a political movement to halt the degradation of life on Earth, to analyze systemic causes and alternatives, and also as a "cognitive revolution and spiritual awakening" that amounts to "a shift in our sense of identity" as humans, reawakening a numbed-out consciousness of ourselves as part of the web of life.[5] In *The Great Turning*, David C. Korten described it not as prophecy but "a possibility," that possibility being to live in democratic partnership with one another and the living Earth.[6]

I too think of it as a possibility, one that must be chosen and actively cultivated, though I'd call it a turn toward *implicated participation*. I take this term from time theorist Barbara Adam, who contrasted the ordered rationality of clock time to the time of life unfolding in the budding of a flower or of a smile on a person's face. "We are time," she reminded us.[7] The challenge is to live this way, not just executing tasks with nanosecond efficiency, but being alive to the here and now, being able to dwell in the moment, attuned to the pulse of life and the rhythm of relationships, ready to be accountable, an implicated participant in life. Or, as Adam put it in *Timewatch: The Social Analysis of Time*, "we need to highlight the creativity of the implicated participant, of the embedded, embodied maker of ... global futures."[8] As I see it, the shift involved is simultaneously personal and political. It's about healing — healing the disconnect in ourselves, from ourselves and one another and from the Earth. It's also about institutional transformation and political change, enacting a broadly based claim to act as participants in commons — social and natural habitats — locally, regionally, nationally and globally. The commons practices and related spiritual ones from the past can serve to guide and inspire this movement on every level on which movement must occur. This includes at the level of knowledge and knowing, and this in turn includes being able to name and know what's real in terms that matter to us all.

This ability to name and know galvanized the women who launched the Idle No More Movement in Canada in 2012. They read the Canadian federal government's omnibus bill C-45 (known as the *Jobs and Growth Act, 2012*), cutting through the spin in the title and the volumes of legalese. They clearly named the reality at work as a violation of both a social contract (treaty rights) and a covenant with land that, for them, is their inherited sacred duty to protect. The change in the wording of just one of the hundreds of laws affected by the omnibus legislation said it all: what had been the *Navigable Waters Protection Act* would become the *Navigation Protection Act*. The word water had been removed. In keeping with this change, only waterways listed by the Canadian Minister of Transport were henceforth to be protected. The women launching Idle No More claimed that this change left 99% of Canada's lakes and rivers with no one to speak for and protect them. This, to them, was unacceptable. It was and is to me as well.

And so I went to Victoria Island in Ottawa, Ontario, through late December 2012 and early January 2013, taking food and firewood to the supporters of Chief Theresa Spence in her hunger strike, and I marched with Idle No More demonstrators on Parliament Hill. And through it all, I continued to find my way in the journey that is this book. It's my way of trying to walk beside these people who were the first inhabitants of the land I now call home. I can't walk their path. But I can find and follow a parallel path. I can continue this journey I've begun, as someone who is non-native to North America and yet has an indigenous past and chooses to honor it. By reconnecting with the traditions of my past, I am finding my own way to reconnect with the Earth and to form common cause with movements like Idle No More. If we do come together as kindred spirits and allies, perhaps we can articulate a new social contract that is simultaneously a covenant with Creation, replacing an ethic of domination with an ethic of mutual respect and coexistence.

None of this will be easy. I look around as I think this, and nearly burst out laughing. I'm now sitting in the departure lounge of the Philadelphia airport waiting for my connecting flight home to Ottawa, but I could be anywhere. There's the usual array of fast-food outlets where staff have look-alike uniforms, sound-alike scripts and operating procedures. Scanning the crowd, I see a few people talking among themselves. More than half, though, are plugged into their own wired world, ears tuned into their own soundscape, eyes focused on their portable electronic devices, the multiple screens of their server's delivery systems. They're like astronauts in space suits doing a space walk, totally enclosed in their technological world and its support structures. This simultaneous electronic isolation and connection is another enclosure movement, and I've witnessed its unfolding over my lifetime as well. I've also chronicled its downside in stress and disconnection from the body and from others, and in compulsive multitasking, even addiction to being on and online all the time. In my book *No Time*, I began a section on what I called "the attention deficit culture" with a look at the seeming epidemic of kids being diagnosed with attention deficit disorder (ADD). This is partly because too many parents these days are too busy and distracted to give their infants the sustained, focused loving attention babies need to establish essential neural patterns for relating to others and, with them, the patterns of connection.[9] In other words, the issue isn't present or future displacement but a relative absence of emplacement in the first place.

I sigh and get up, sling my backpack in place and join the line to board the last leg of my flight home. The work of reconnection is vast and huge, including the work of choosing it. It will take a lot of healing and, with that, capacity building. It will require learning or relearning the language of the common good, and rebuilding responsible self-governance from institution to institution, and from the community up. It will take time to build the base for a movement, a polycentric grassroots movement, to reclaim the commons of both the social and natural environment. And throughout, it will also require a choice made again and again and again: the choice of connection with Earth and with each other and, with this, a commitment to stay the course in the face of the global economy, with its ceaseless novelty and distractions.

In the next chapters of Part II, I explore ways that the self-organizing, self-governing, self-informing commons can guide and inspire us to build new capacities. I begin with a brief account of my involvement in the Gabriola Commons, a living experiment in reviving a commons community in the 21st century, because it's a good way to introduce themes of capacity building I will explore. The first is the capacity to connect with one's self and others and, from there, to connect with nature. The capacity to show up, to be present, ready to be implicated in what's going on here and now could be the most critical piece in the work of reclaiming the commons and a sense of ourselves as part of it. Chapters 14 and 15 focus on knowledge: Chapter 14 on reviving the capacity to know through connection and implicated participation and Chapter 15 on developing a knowledge commons from which a new common sense on actionable priorities can emerge. Chapter 16 explores building commons-like organizational capacity and an ethos of the common good, while Chapter 17 talks about renewing a sense of the sacred and of our place in Creation. We won't restore balance to our social and natural environments out of utilitarian rationality, though rational arguments have their place. Reclaiming the commons requires reviving a feeling for our implicated place within it.

Reclaiming the Commons on Gabriola Island

I'M ALWAYS AT EASE WHEN I ARRIVE for a Saturday morning work bee at the Gabriola Commons. I'm not in charge, nor is anyone else. So I don't need to wait for instruction. I simply pay attention to the patterns forming as people mill about, looking at the list of work that needs doing. It's handwritten on the white board outside what had been once a goat barn. I watch as people team up around projects that strike them as most urgent, or simply strike their fancy, and then I join in. We collect what tools we need from the Commons tool shed, and head out in groups of three or four. Some might be digging a trench to lay down more irrigation piping for the allotment gardens in the bottom land by the pond where the soil is deepest and most fertile. Others might be pruning apple trees or weeding the new plantation of haskaps (*Lonicera caerulea L.*), a blueberry-like fruit rich in antioxidants, while others work donated manure or vegetable scraps into the compost bins.

Two hours later, we hear the clanging of metal on metal that signals "Soup's On," and we gather in the former farmhouse on the property for a lunch of hearty soup and usually homemade bread. Boots by the door, we wander around in sock feet filling our bowls, buttering the bread, putting out mugs for tea, filling glasses with water. Then we crowd around the table and settle to the serious business of filling our hungry stomachs and talking. Conversation ranges from the politics of the wider world to the details of the work we've all just been doing. Observations are shared, stories told bringing on laughter and more stories. Questions are explored, advice sought and given. And in the comfortable quiet of the post-meal cleanup, I find myself thinking: this is the commons; I sense its ethos rising.

In less than ten years, the financial legacy of a dying man has become a thriving community within the community of Gabriola, a small island off the coast of British Columbia, Canada, with a population of around 4,000. It embodies what activist geographers champion as "participatory spaces of action that are inclusive and non-hierarchical"[1] and at least one community development theorist has identified as the "entrepreneurial social infrastructure"[2] that community-based action requires.

In a sense, the idea of The Gabriola Commons dates back to 1995 when a planning study by the local regional government (District of Nanaimo) identified a 26-acre former goat farm on Gabriola as ideally sited for a future community center. The land, which is a mix of fields, forest and wetlands with some buildings close to the road, is conveniently located next to both the commercial hub of the island and two important public institutions — the elementary school and a seniors' center. To lay the groundwork, the land was zoned for community-focused purposes, its use designated as "not-for-profit." But no community center was built, perhaps because there is no local government on the island to take the initiative. Instead, initiative was seized by local citizens, specifically two women on the board of the Amazing Grace Ecological Society (AGES) that was created in 2004 to apply what money long-time Gabriola resident Jay Mussell would leave on his death from cancer to advance his vision of a peaceful and sustainable world. The two women were Heide Brown, a permaculturalist, and Shelagh Huston, an economist and a long-time supporter of Elinor Ostrom's work on the commons in the modern era. A year later, AGES bought the goat farm, using Jay's money to make a sizeable down payment. An initial steering committee, all community members and volunteers, met biweekly to learn about land use bylaws and what models of governance might work best, to explore conservation policy and strategies for mobilizing funds both for operating expenses and for paying off the mortgage. By 2007, the committee had approval from the provincial Agricultural Land Commission to submit an application to the Islands Trust (a provincial body governing land use issues on BC's Gulf Islands, including Gabriola) to create a new zoning bylaw appropriate for an institution "where sustainability, community and agriculture meet" in the words of the application — i.e. one that combined people, land and community land use almost as an indivisible whole, in keeping with the original meaning of the common. In 2010, two new Islands Trust bylaws were passed. One, #258, officially established and defined for the first time in Canada a "community commons;" the second, bylaw #259, officially recognized the Gabriola Commons as a Comprehensive Development Zone in its own right. In January 2011, these bylaws were approved by the provincial government. A premodern institution had been revived in the postmodern era in a country where such an institution had never been formally recognized before.

The initial Commons steering committee has evolved into a set of self-directed teams, each representing its own circle of autonomous action and information sharing, but also nested within larger circles, the first being the Commons Coordinating Council, where the teams report at monthly meetings and discuss issues of general interest. These meetings are open to the whole community, including the media. The teams include:

+ a farm management team that coordinates both the individual allotment gardens and the more farm-related projects like the apple orchard, the haskaps and growing heritage seed potatoes — in keeping with the Commons land being designated for agriculture
+ a special-events team that organizes such community-wide projects as a Fall Fair, Spring Seed Exchange, concerts and other cultural events

+ a facilities-upkeep team that looks after the grounds and buildings and helps support Saturday morning work bees
+ a sharing-the-commons team that intentionally fosters access to the Commons and collaboration across other institutions on Gabriola
+ a trails and green spaces team that protects the forest and wetlands, and eradicates invasive species.
+ a covenant team that's developing a unique covenant for the Commons that combines nature and culture in a frame of conservation, bridging modernity's long-standing divide that has resulted in a purist biocentric view of conservation (in which humans are assumed to be bad and needing to be excluded).

The Gabriola Commons Foundation and Board of Trustees comprise another team. It is the formal, legal landowner (holding the land on behalf of the community). It also oversees financial management and ensures that all the actions and decisions taken by all the teams are accountable to the principles and commitments of the Commons to which larger governance bodies, including a covenant holder, will hold the Commons accountable.

This team structure is the first set of circles in a "polycentric" model of governance championed by commons theorists.[3] Instead of a remote central government controlling and managing everything, control and decision-making responsibility are decentered. A meaningful measure of self-governing autonomy resides in the council, board and work teams of the Commons. In return for being accountable to the more remote government authority to honor prevailing standards and policy principles, the Commons' authority to act locally in the public interest is both recognized and backed by larger government bodies. The Gabriola Commons hasn't evolved yet to the point that specific self-governing areas of authority are named as in a federal constitution. However, the Commons Charter and Covenant are steps in that direction. The

Charter sets out five guiding principles for the Commons, starting with public trust: that the Gabriola Commons is a public trust and "exists in perpetuity for the benefit of the land and the people of Gabriola ... not favouring one generation over another." The other principles include ecological and social sustainability, local democracy and community engagement. The Covenant takes this further, especially as the team involved seeks an outside public body (and possibly more than one) to act as covenant holder, overseeing that the institutional practices of the Commons, as well as the land itself are conserved. I sit part time on the team that's trying to craft appropriate words and metaphors to break the mould of conventional covenants associated with strictly land conservation, and bridge the culture-nature divide. The preamble we drafted begins: "The Gabriola Commons is an ongoing, reciprocal relationship; the people care for the Land and the Land nurtures the people." Section 3, setting out the Intent of the Covenant, begins by stating that first, the intent is "to advance certain principles and practices that will expand conventional understandings of conservation to include cultural dimensions, by applying the following ideas:

> 3.1.1 that Commons activities bring the people of Gabriola together on the Land working in shared purpose without expectation of compensation;
> 3.1.2 that this be achieved through open communication and principles of reciprocity, in keeping with historical precedents of self-governing commons;
> 3.1.3 that solidarity between the community members and the Land strengthens capacity for biospheric and social ethics as well as sustainability in both spheres;"[4]

All this is far more easily said than done, of course, though even pulling those words into shape took many long meetings spread over about three years. The reality is that transformation takes time, and the commons is a work of transformation. The Gabriola Commons website describes the commons as "a grassroots community organization, managed by volunteers...; "[5] those words alone have lots of baggage. For many people, community still means what it came to mean in the modern era of the nation-state: a largely "imagined" community of shared symbols in the words of one theorist, and also organizations of "horizontal comradeship."[6] The word community organization often means a civic institution, a center delivering services. People are used to the idea of finding certain things on offer when they arrive, things they can consume, not things that they have to co-create.

The Gabriola Commons, however, is a community and community center that exists only through the collective actions of the people who happen to show up, everyone doing their share. Moreover, the actions involve direct relations with the land of the Commons. So this Commons, like the premodern commons of my ancestors, is a community embedded in the land, a matrix of relationships that entwine the social and the natural environment into a together-as-one habitat through a mix of symbolic and physical actions. It's a habitat too that has to be steadily coproduced over time in order for it to become real. Its health and fecundity are growing in lockstep with the community of people who are associating themselves with it. Therefore the people making it real aren't so much volunteers. They are implicated participants.

One challenge of being an implicated participant, versus merely a volunteer, is simply showing up on a regular basis to sustain the commoning action. Another is getting used to responsibility and power. People who become involved in the Commons are often deeply steeped in hierarchy, representative authority and delegated power. They're used to either being in charge or being told what to do. Things at least are clear that way; it's easy to get on with things. Not so on the Commons where everything is decided by teams, and the teams are run through direct, participatory democracy. All this takes time and patience, and the habits of attentive listening, humility and negotiating differences respectfully. There are occasionally freeloaders, bullies and sneaky passive-aggressive types. What to do? There is no rescue. There are no answers. The Gabriola Commons could fail because of this. If it does, it will be a breakdown or failure to develop the necessary trust and mutual recognition, the ethos of the commons and the common good. So far, the Commons is in fact succeeding.[7]

This Commons might also fail at the levels of knowledge and the capacity to trust local, experience-based knowledge and to do the work of testing and consolidating this as authoritative common knowledge, which isn't easy. Just as most people are used to hierarchy and designated authority, most of us are also used to experts knowing what to do and telling us what to do. Taking up the responsibility and work of being an attentive participant, of each of us contributing our share of information and knowledge to collective decision-making, is hard. Often people second-guess themselves, disparage their experience and observations because they don't have what they consider to be the relevant credentials. And they disappear themselves a little each time they do this, discrediting their own importance in the commoning effort. Yet, again, the experience at the Commons has been heartening, with people's self-confidence growing as they participate in meetings and work bees, sharing experience with others.[8]

It's impossible to predict whether the Gabriola Commons will succeed, drawing in a critical mass of Gabriola residents who claim it as part of their lives and their sense of shared local identity. There's no predicting either whether it will fulfill the promise of the premodern commons that was simultaneously community, ecology and economy. Still, the possibility is there in the carefully preserved bottom-land pond, the boardwalk trails through the woods, in the allotment gardens, the apple and nut groves, the blueberry and haskap fields, the weekly work bees, the seed-exchange Saturdays, and at the spring and the fall fairs, in the community garden from which fresh vegetables flow to the food bank located on the premises and the Community Kitchen being set up in the former goat barn. This kitchen will be run as a cooperative, with any Gabriola individual or family being able to use its facilities to preserve their own food and community groups, to prepare food for community cultural events and so on. Such a community-embedded, cost-recovery social enterprise might help renew a model of local economy to help offset the near monopoly of the market economy: an economy embedded in social relations and the land, not transactional relations and the market.

A lot of capacity building and a lot of healing will be required if such a commons and similar initiatives are to flourish and make a difference.

Capacity Building #1 — Healing and Connecting with Our Selves

T HE WORD COMMON MEANS "TOGETHER IN ONE" while the verb form, commoning, means sharing and participating in fellowship, in communion and community.[1] Yet so many people have lost or don't have that capacity for coming together except at the fungible, fleeting level of online connectivity. They are "alone together" as Sherry Turkle put it in her 2011 book by that title, referring to people with fingers and eyes on their portable devices and essentially absent even when they are present in the same room. The fourth book in a series this MIT-based psychoanalyst has written probing the promise and dangers of computer connections, *Alone Together* raised serious questions about people's capacity for sustained relationships with others and even for a mature and stable sense of self. Turkle's research is echoed in reports of loneliness reaching almost epidemic proportions. Two studies in the US reported that 40% of people describe themselves as lonely, a figure that's doubled in 30 years. In Canada, a 2012 survey of Vancouver residents listed social isolation as their most pressing concern.[2] Turkle's research also built on a 2010 University of Michigan study of college students chronicling a growing "empathy deficit" among heavy users of electronic devices, who were more likely to admit that 'other people's misfortunes' usually don't disturb them.[3] Turkle shed light on this as she chronicled emergent patterns among the first and second Internet generation of young people, including a "multitasking high," and "hyper-other directedness" with a hunger for connection readily interrupted by the promise of a next connection. Through it all, Turkle observed, there's a tendency "to treat those we meet online in something of the same way we treat objects — with dispatch[4] — much as so many people in the job market are treated these days of fleeting, part-time, term and contract employment.

For most of my career as a writer and conference speaker, I did much the same thing, even as I deplored the way the economy was dispatching people, their skills, their experience and their dreams. I engaged with people whose jobs were being lost or whose knowledge was being black-boxed. I gave them a moment of instant empathy — if that's not an oxymoron. And I moved on. I was always on the move. I had to be if I wanted to keep up with the morphing of the debate. It was safe for me, too, to stay at cruising altitude so to speak. I was above it all, the expert, the global activist, not the local one bogged down in the messy business of working things out together, the necessary daily legwork of commoning, coming together-as-one. I even admitted to being a workaholic, knowing that this was socially acceptable, almost a badge of honor on the global conference circuit. I didn't own up to the kind of negative things that were chronicled in a 2011 National College Health Assessment survey. Among the 1,600 University of Alberta students surveyed, 87% reported feeling exhausted, 61% reported feeling very lonely and 52% felt overwhelming anxiety.[5] It took years of counseling for the penny to drop for me, that my frantic busyness might be an addiction.

In *The Globalization of Addiction*, psychologist Bruce Alexander did not rank or even draw distinctions among addictions be they to work, to wealth and power, to pornography, online shopping, gaming or gambling, self-improvement, cruising or social networking. He included all these with the familiarly labeled addictions to drugs and alcohol because in his view all addictions are the same beneath the surface. They're united by the same compulsive drive: an overwhelming involvement in this activity, a narcissistic self-absorption around it. It's a coping mechanism for an absence of what psychologists call "psycho-social integration" in community, which a long line of psychologists, including Erik Erikson, have argued is essential to a secure sense of self. Alexander made a compelling case for the enduring human need for community and belonging, drawing even on Charles Darwin for support. Darwin might be known for seeming to champion competitive individualism. But he also argued that humans are innately drawn to community, innately inclined to feel sympathy for their neighbors and to cooperate. In Alexander's account, Darwin ranked this social instinct on a par with the competitive instinct, saying that evolution is the working out of the tension and conflict between them, with that tension a creative requirement for evolution.[6]

The loss or absence of this engaged sense of participating in community, through displacement, dislocation, disconnection and alienation, is the crux of much theorizing about the roots of addiction, including Alexander's. Dr. Gabor Maté, a Canadian doctor specializing in addiction, added importantly to this by drawing in the literature on brain development in infancy to highlight the danger if the pathways for connection and integration with others in community aren't given a chance to develop. "Human connections create neuronal connections," Maté cited child psychiatrist and founding member of UCLA's Center for Culture, Brain and Development as saying, augmenting this with his own observations about the critical importance of foundational early childhood relationships, relationships of attuned attachment, attention and connection.[7] He would doubtless agree with Alexander who argued that dislocation and addiction are mass produced by our multitasking, free-market society.

In *The Globalization of Addiction*, Alexander devoted considerable space to the dislocation associated with the Highland Clearances and the widespread drunkenness that emerged in their wake. This addiction to alcohol was carried across the Atlantic among the displaced Scots who found work with the Hudson's Bay Company. Alexander wrote at length too about addiction in native communities, especially in his home province of British Columbia, Canada where, he argued, dislocation happened more abruptly and more recently. He also talked about addiction in the broader population, linking it to emotional isolation, powerlessness and stress.

On reading Alexander's book, I wondered about me, four generations removed from the terrible disruption that brought my people to Canada in the early 1840s. Do I carry their dislocation in my genes like some torn umbilical cord of family memory? Perhaps it was transmuted through the hardships they endured. One branch of my great-grandparents tried cattle ranching in the near-desert dry lands of southern Texas and failed, while another felled trees and homesteaded, like Susannah Moodie, in what was for them the wilderness of Western Ontario (then Upper Canada). My parents grew up in the Depression and survived the traumas of World War II, both serving overseas. My mother was in London during the Blitz, helping to run a Red Cross canteen. My father was with the Black Watch during the blood-soaked liberation of Holland. Both also lost their mothers when they were very young, experiencing the primal displacement that this entails. Both kept themselves very busy most of the time, inculcating a work ethic in their children that has served us all well, yet at considerable cost.

I think back to my father and how much he slowed down when he got to the farm on the weekend, tense and stressed from his job as a senior executive in the Montreal branch of a British multinational. He threw himself into the hard physical work the place demanded, and by Sunday I could tell he had come back home to himself and to us, the family he loved so much. Now I think about myself, and how I've driven myself over the years, first to be credited as an expert on technological change and then to keep myself on the speaking circuit, a new book in print every few years to keep myself up to date and in demand. In the last book of that series, looking at living in an online world, I worried about the implications of people multitasking their way through their days, a bit present here and there, but fully present nowhere. I documented people's increasing dependency on the screen not just for "expected outcomes" and "performance measures" but generally too for cues and direction on what was real and relevant. I explored the consequences of this: an infant left to die of starvation in Toronto when officially under state care while the people in charge played telephone tag and documented missed appointments in computerized logs of accountability. The reality on screens effectively obscured lived reality.[8] And yet at the time, I was living the disconnect that I was working so hard to describe in others.

Now I'm trying to live the reconnect, and taking my time to do this book right has been part of it. But living the reconnect is not just a one-off project on my to-do list; it's an ongoing process and commitment. This means I have to watch the pace at which I'm living, constantly. I have to keep choosing to be connected with myself and others, and to stay present to myself and others with whom I work, share a coffee or go for a walk. At the same time, I have to keep resisting the hyper activity of 24-7 digital connectivity. I have to be "mindful," as they say in Buddhist practice, doing things that will bring me home to myself, every day — things that will slow me down — things like gardening, walking, swimming, cooking meals from scratch, even putting laundry on the line (I'm fortunate enough to have one) and bringing it back in smelling of billowing fresh air. I practice meditation too, and have learned the hard way that it's the practice that's critical. It has to be daily to make a difference, to cultivate that inward habitat of calm that calls me home to myself, back to grounded connection. It took counseling to help me get to this place, to take me off the hook of having to always be performing and producing, staying online to stay in the loop. Being busy all the time numbed out my underlying insecurities and inner loneliness, and it took a while to break the habit and begin to find my way home. Still, having begun that work, having developed the practice, I'm also tapping into its benefits. The more I'm securely connected to myself, the more I can risk connecting with others, getting involved in the Gabriola Commons, committing to endless meetings of the Covenant Team. I'm reconstituting the habitat of the commons within myself.

13

Capacity Building #2 — Healing, Habitats and Reconnecting with Nature

WHAT I'VE LEARNED ABOUT ENVIRONMENT ASTOUNDS ME. It's not something out there; it's here and all around me. We each live in our own microenvironment, our own personal habitat. We also co-create this; all organisms do, according to developmental geneticist Richard Lewontin. As he put it in *Biology as Ideology*, "there is no 'environment' in some independent and abstract sense. Just as there is no organism without an environment, there is no environment without an organism. Organisms don't experience environments. They create them."[1] Birds do this by collecting twigs, bits of plastic and mud to build a nest, and people do it through material things like clothes and furniture and immaterial things like daily habits and practices. Teenagers can create at least something of a personal habitat when they withdraw behind hoodies or unconventional clothes, body piercings and makeup, keeping sound buds in their ears, eyes and fingers on their digital devices.

The human microenvironment is perhaps the most important to understand considering that 90% of human brain circuitry is wired after birth — with early life experience causing some neurons and synapses to grow and others not.[2] This is a new understanding, even a new paradigm, in neuroscience. It replaces the old deterministic view that genes controlled brain development completely with a view suggesting that genes only set out possibilities. How these possibilities or potentials are expressed largely depends on the environment within which a child grows up,[3] an environment that parents, teachers and other caregivers help to coproduce. Given this, one thing is also clear: if we are to have any hope of renewing a consciousness of ourselves as commoners, together-as-one with the Earth and with each other in community, the cultivation of early childhood connections is crucial.

And right now this isn't happening, according to Richard Louv, author of *Last Child in the Woods*. Most North American children these days are being raised in cities or massive subdivisions far from the chance not just to connect with nature but to enter some kind of meaningful relationship with the elements of it they find there: shrubs and trees, frogs in a creek. They need to be involved, he argued, exploring and making themselves familiar with some local bit of forest, meadow or marsh, quoting Frank Wilson, a professor of neurology at Stanford University School of Medicine. Wilson studied the coevolution of the hominid hand and brain, concluding that each helped the other to evolve. "We've been sold a bill of goods — especially parents — about how valuable computer-based experience is," Wilson wrote in *The Hand*. "We are creatures identified by what we do with our hands."[4] But instead of children climbing trees and mucking about, Louv found in his research, they are at best merely spectators in nature. Between 1997 and 2003, there was a 50% decline in the proportion of American children aged 9 to 12 who engage in outdoor activities like hiking, gardening, fishing or beach play. There's also been a huge drop in the numbers of families going to nature and wilderness parks. Another study found that children's free play time had dropped by 9 hours a week over the past 25 years. As well, Louv wrote, children are growing up no longer connecting food in the supermarket with its origins in the soil, another telling symptom. All in all, he wrote, childhood has become denatured, and the consequences are troubling. Not only does Louv embrace the biophilia theory of Harvard scientist Edward O. Wilson who argued that humans have an innate affinity for the natural world, and need

that connection to feel whole. Louv endorsed Theodore Roszak's interpretation of the American Psychiatric Association's understanding of
"separation anxiety disorder" as including the natural as well as social
environment. "[N]o separation is more pervasive in this Age of Anxiety
than our disconnection from the natural world," Roszak wrote.[5] Louv
coined the phrase *nature deficit disorder* to summarize research docu-
menting the costs of this disconnect, this "alienation from nature" as he
put it. The costs include attention difficulties, diminished use of the
senses and higher rates of physical and emotional illness.

Louv quoted medical researchers in Seattle who found that by 3
months of age, some 40% of kids were regularly watching TV, DVDs
or other videos.[6] In my own book *No Time*, I cited statistics on ADD
and quoted various sources including Gabor Maté who linked this both
to too much early immersion in a quick-click, flitting-image media environment and to not enough grounding in attuned, mutually attentive
relationships. I excavated the meaning of the word "attention," derived
from Latin words *ad* and *tendere*, meaning "to reach toward." In other
words, attention is an act of seeking and sustaining connection. I also
tracked down the Canadian woman, Virginia Douglas, who'd first identified the phenomenon known as ADD associated with kids having
problems at school. ADD is characterized by fragmented, disorganized
behavior linked to an underlying problem of short, flitting attention, an
inability to stay focused and sustain concentrated attention. It's really a
"self-regulatory disorder," Virginia Douglas told me.[7]

In *Alone Together*, Sherry Turkle talked about "'post-familial families'" whose members are "each in their own rooms, each on a networked
computer or mobile device." Speaking of the parents who have co-cre-
ated this habitat for their children, she reported that "as we, ourselves
enchanted, turned away from them to lose ourselves in our e-mail, we
did not sufficiently teach the importance of empathy and attention
to what is real." Turkle expressed concerns about not only the online
world of hyperactivity but its increasing population by sociable robots
that replace real-life friends and confidantes. "Overwhelmed, we have
been drawn to connections that seem low risk and always at hand:

Facebook friends, avatars, IRC chat partners."[8] In a footnote, Turkle mentioned a study that documented a steady decline (between 1985 and 2004) in the number of people with whom Americans can discuss matters important to them, with the number of people who reported having no one to confide in more than doubling to 25%.[9] This study supports other studies chronicling the rise of isolation and depression among young people.[10] Turkle also cited a marginal note written by Erik Erikson in a book called *The Protean Self* written by one of Erikson's students, Robert Jay Lifton. Where Lifton had written enthusiastically about an emergent "protean man," Erikson had penned in the margin: "protean boy?"[11] In other words, Turkle interpreted Erikson's query as meaning "terminally juvenile," unequipped and unfit for the responsibilities of mature adulthood not just as parents but as implicated participants in society.

To offset our isolation from one another requires a second area of capacity building: sharing grounded connection not just with our children but with the Earth, the habitat from which all life derives. If we are to learn and teach our children to be stewards of the larger commons and environment, we must first be responsible for those we co-create in our homes and local communities. "Environments" condition and shape us. They enable some things and disable others. It's what Marshall McLuhan meant in his famous aphorism "the medium is the message," inspiring a whole new school of communication called "media ecology" that focuses on the social relations of communication and the larger medium context. McLuhan actually spelled this out once, explaining that when he coined this memorable phrase, he meant that media function as environments. The infrastructure and operating atmosphere and environment of a particular medium work people over, he said, imparting and implanting a message far deeper and more lasting than any messages carried through its structures.[12] It's the relationship, detached or intimate, observer or participant within the environment that matters.

I learned this as a child, both at the farm planting trees and in the backyard garden at our suburban home tending the vegetables and weeding. I learned it more fully as a mother, whole conversations with my infant son unfolding through eye contact, body language and pre-verbal exchanges of sounds. And I learned it in the classroom teaching seminar courses for some 20 years at Carleton University where I capped enrollments if I could to ensure a rich and inclusive dialogue with everyone around the table. In all cases, the important thing was being fully present, relating to others and other life forms, co-creating an environment of mutuality, learning and growth.

I have kept up gardening ever since childhood, raising my family almost entirely on my backyard garden's produce. Even in the days when I lived in an apartment, I kept it up, renting space in allotment gardens run by the City of Winnipeg when I lived there and, later, Ottawa. Once I grew lettuce and arugala in an old wooden drawer I'd salvaged. I've always liked having my hands in the dirt, forking in compost that I've managed to make myself, marking off rows and planting seeds one by one, covering them with earth and patting that into place, then waiting for the first telltale crack in the earth, the pale shaft of a seedling poking through, seeking the sun. Often I work the garden barefoot, and having now read William Bryant Logan's book *Dirt: The Ecstatic Skin of the Earth*, I do so with an added delight and intent. Logan's book contains a wealth of fascinating facts, my favorite being that as people work skin to skin with their hands in the dirt, it boosts their serotonin levels.[13]

Small wonder, I think as I consider that working the soil this way, day after day, week after week through the summer is also a way of relating to the Earth directly and even intimately. I come to know it as I turn it over with a shovel or fork, my nose taking in small shifts in smell, my fingers absorbing subtle shifts in texture. The soil is alive to me, and I to it. A relationship has been formed; the biochemical reaction is surely merely a sign.

But this is only part of what's needed. It's important to share this, through community gardens or working out the sharing of water and tools in allotment gardens. It's the sharing of this embedded physical work, and the organizational details around it, that fosters a social as well as natural habitat. Part of capacity building, then, is recognizing many existing sites, institutions and community projects as possible commons-like habitats that can be coproduced by people through the activities they're involved in. In existing social habitats (community centers, schools, churches, for example) further capacity building might involve building relationships with the outdoors. A church might sponsor an outdoor community labyrinth, a mosque, a halal chicken coop. A school and community center might cosponsor a community vegetable garden. Alternately, where the habitat is largely natural (such as a nature conservancy) capacity building here might mean building social relationships by, for example, constructing a boardwalk through a wetland, creating signs to illustrate a walking tour or forming a partnership with a local mental health facility through which clients can participate in green therapy.

At its simplest, a *commons* is a habitat of interrelationships, bound by mutuality: mutual obligation and mutual self-interest and also, hopefully, affinity. The Gabriola Commons is an emergent expression of such integrated capacity building. People decide things together, and they do things together on the land. Relationships are formed, even *right relations* involving mutual recognition and respect toward both other people and other lifeforms. Trust is developed. People become implicated participants, more and more immersed in what's going on, attuned to the pulse of ongoing growth. And as they do, an ethos is developing, the beginnings of what might one day be called a *commons consciousness*. Part of this is coming to know things together as well, with the resultant knowledge informing self-governing decision-making and fostering the confidence that together-as-one, we can get things done.

14

Capacity Building #3 — Ecoliteracy and Knowing through Implicated Participation

W HAT IS CREDITED AND FRAMED AS REAL, AND BY WHOM, strongly influences what can or cannot be done, and what will be done. This is the reason that so many people interested in societal change also call for a change in our thinking and knowing. As Boaventura de Sousa Santos, one of the founders of the World Social Forum, put it: "Global cognitive justice is essential if global social justice is to be achieved."[1] Global environmental justice too, I would add. Some ways of knowing enfranchise people in the here and now of a situation, the inhabitants of a habitat and the habitat itself, while other ways almost disappear them. Some ways of knowing enfranchise those designated as authorities — official observers, reporters and experts — who are necessarily removed from the situation in the interests of so-called objectivity. Cognitive and epistemological justice requires a perspective balanced between insider and outsider, practices of implicated participation dating back to premodernity and modern ones of remote observation.

I presumed that my ancestors practiced premodern ways on the commons of the Scottish Highlands. But I had no way of really understanding what these ways entailed until I read British anthropologist Tim Ingold's acclaimed *The Perception of the Environment*. The book critiques conventional anthropological wisdom which depicted pre-modern, Neolithic people through the modern lens as "backward," at a "primitive" stage on the ladder of progress and development. It also showcases work attempting to reverse this bias and understand such people on their own terms. This reversal means honoring these others as being on their own, different path of development, perhaps geared primarily to the full and healthy development of life, not the production of things for profit. Essentially, Ingold argued, Neolithic people (which included hunter-farmers like my forbears) came to know and relate to their environment as living participants in it, not remotely through observation and expert analysis. Theirs was and in some places still is participatory knowledge, all of a piece with a participatory consciousness of reality. There being no word in Cree for nature, nor, for that matter, for culture is not a lapse in the development and consciousness of Cree people, Ingold pointed out. It's indicative of a highly evolved, if different, consciousness. Within such consciousness, the mind is not displaced from either the body or from the experienced world. It's "immanent," said Ingold. Mind is an aspect of intentional engagement, and so is credible knowledge.[2]

Ingold called this participatory posture a "dwelling" or "dwelt-in," and sometimes simply an "engaged" or "immersed" perspective. To understand people who live this way on their own terms, he wrote, "… it is imperative to take this condition of involvement as our point of departure."[3]

A dwelling or engaged perspective is the crux of traditional knowledge, and the kind of knowing that needs to be revived. It takes a stance of what I call implicated participation. One knows by relating to what you're working with or otherwise encountering and connecting with, knowing with open eyes and even a listening, empathetic heart. It's not so much "I know" from afar as almost "I know you," or "I care about you enough to want to understand what you know."[4] And so, in Ingold's words: "one gets to know the forest, and the plants and animals that dwell therein, in just the same way that one becomes familiar with other people, by spending time with them, investing in one's relations with them the same qualities of care, feeling and attention."[5]

I recall that potent phrase, a field in good heart, from the literature on the premodern, self-governing, self-determining, self-informing commons. I now also realize that the point of this knowing, or knowing in this way, was to sustain that field, to sustain the relationships that sustained the life of the common community. My ancestors' knowing was tied to the well-being of the common and all its occupants, human and non-human, not just to what could be extracted from it (which the Improvers promoted). This profound difference in knowing is probably at least one reason why the commoners were excluded from debates about the Enclosure of the Commons. It was convenient to dismiss people like my ancestors as ignorant because they were illiterate. It was convenient to focus the debate on knowledge vested in texts, shared in the elite halls of Oxford University and Parliament and produced by modern scientists, including thinkers like John Locke. These experts were flag bearers of the Agricultural Revolution, the productivity of which supplied the emergent modern commercial markets of the day. It was convenient to discuss growing things within the frame of this new science of economics, which took producing for markets and the "law" of supply and demand running them as the norm.

Dismissing the immersed, dwelling perspective hid the shift in mind-set, worldview and prevailing ideology that was going on: a shift from a society and economy embedded in social relations and relations with the land to a society and economy centered in the market and the utilitarian logic of maximizing production for market gain. This logic might have falsely been assumed to be universally at play at the time the tragedy of the commons was first predicted nearly 200 years ago. However, it appears to be almost universally at play now, and that's why the tragedy appears to be unfolding as tragedies do, with no other way of knowing and no other logic to stop it. It's become almost trite to say that the larger commons of Earth itself is being pushed beyond its carrying capacity, its capacity to cope and sustain itself, to sustain life in diversity and health. Polar sea ice is melting, oceans are becoming more acidic, sea and air currents are being pushed off their age-old patterns. And the carbon intensity of the atmosphere and its median temperature are rising inexorably toward the doomsday thresholds that will tip the paradigm, unleashing irreversible devastation.[6]

Part of this unstoppability lies in the huge concentration of monopoly-scale vested interest around the status quo of continued market growth and investment, with vast infrastructures of global transportation and communication, of finance, investment, insurance, brokerage as well as production, marketing and consumption, all of them voracious and codependent. So the inertia here is huge.

But monopoly-scale structures of knowledge are also key, especially to the seeming inevitability of it all. It's not just that official circles where the issues are discussed are dominated by experts accountable to the institutions that employ or fund them, and that many of these institutions, including governments, are committed ideologically to the global market and its continued expansion for the sake of jobs and social stability. Nor is it just that many of the credentialed knowers — scientists — are being thwarted in their work by gag orders and funding cuts. It's that we continue to exclude any knowing vested in the experience of life immersed in the environments of Earth. It's that we exclude the kind of knowledge and practices my ancestors relied on to make decisions about the common good and the good of the commons. These inclusive, democratic, participatory, engaged and implicated practices are still valued by Indigenous peoples, but so discredited and marginalized outside these communities that they've been virtually forgotten. One result has been poignantly summarized by American novelist Marilynne Robinson in a powerful book of philosophy called *Absence of Mind.* "A central tenet of the modern world view is that we do not know our own minds.... And — an important corollary — certain, well-qualified others *do*." As one result, she continued, "the testimony of individual consciousness and experience among us ... has fallen silent."[7]

That silence needs to be broken, at least among those of us wanting to restore health and balance to our planet. Breaking the silence will include a lot of capacity building. It will require that we re-enfranchise ordinary people as knowers and life experience as knowledge, that we all recover practices of embedded knowing and, however inconveniently, insist on their validity. I don't know what this work will specifically entail. What I do know is that a more implicated way of knowing, alive to the real-life context of fields or rivers or other habitats, natural and social, is part of reconnecting with them, and coming to care about their welfare. The capacity to learn, to gain knowledge and insights and to care also comes from becoming connected to the realities of a living habitat, entering a relationship with them. I discovered this as a kid, starting at age 10, as I helped to plant roughly 10,000 young trees every spring at the family farm, and coming to care about them in the process.

After the first spring's planting, I regularly visited the trees on the hillside where we'd dug them in and, after the snow had melted enough so we could return to the farm the following spring, I went walking up the hill to see how they'd survived the winter. But I couldn't find them. Or rather whole stretches of rows were simply gone. They'd disappeared under a swoon of last year's tall grasses and weeds, felled by the winter's cumulative snow. Immediately, I hunched down, took off my mitt and reached my hand into the tangle of grasses. I carefully lifted the grass, laid it aside and dug deeper, dislodging the stem of a burdock plant to discover, beneath it, the bleached-out remains of a spruce seedling. The young tree looked like a worn-down toothbrush, all but a few of its needles gone. What remained was bleached and anemic, possibly dead. I slipped my fingers under the slender length of what would one day be the trunk of a tree far taller than me. I lifted gently, and felt the slight spring of both give and resistance. Not dead yet, I thought, and set to work uncovering others in the line, then moved to the next. Now what? They looked pathetic, flattened by the weight of dead weeds and snow. I looked around. There was no one to tell me what to do, no book to use as reference. Yet somehow I sensed what was needed, and went looking. There was plenty of debris from the remains of dead elm trees at the edge of this former field, plus twigs from hawthorn bushes that had grown up in it after it was abandoned. I broke a piece off a branch of dead elm and, with the other hand, gently lifted one of the seedlings, coaxing it into as much of an upright position as I dared without the risk of snapping it off at the base. Then I wedged the elm stick in place as a prop, adjusted it a bit and let the seedling go. It held for a moment, then slid off its perch, back to the ground where I was sure it would simply die. I tried again, feeling for the torque in the seedling itself, re-positioning the stick to better counter it, and let go again. It stayed put. I took a breath, hardly even aware of how I'd been holding it. I smiled and moved on. Each repetition taught me something, my fingers com-municating their learning to my mind, my mind gaining knowledge as it moved across the terrain, entering it imaginatively, gathering infor-mation from my eyes and my hands, improvising strategies. It was as though I was an apprentice, though without a master craftsperson on hand to guide me, only the situation itself, and the urgency of respond-ing to it.

This intuitive plant tending was hardly Nobel-prize-caliber know-ing, although such intuitive, immersed knowing, a long-standing part of "field research" in science was key to at least one Nobel prize that I know of, and celebrated in a book called, fittingly, *A Feeling for the Organism*.[8] Still, my everyday knowledge and everyday acts of attentive learning counted as knowledge, at least for the survival of the seedlings, for the well-being of the habitat we as a family were trying to restore. Equally to the point, it emerged from my method or knowledge prac-tice. As I wrote in an anthology called *Teaching as Activism: Equity Meets Environmentalism*, the knowledge of what to do came out of the relationship I had with those seedlings. It was knowing as relating, knowing through presence, my mind immanent and alive to what was going on and how I could work with that to help restore balance. It was knowing as an extension of that relationship, growing out of it and, in that growing, affirming the relationship and the reality it embodied. It was knowing as connection, as an implicated participant, and in the ac-tions I took acquiring and applying that knowledge, I affirmed myself as an agent of change in this place, this habitat,[9] and accountable to it too. In the theorizing words of J.K. Gibson-Graham, co-authors of *A Postcapitalist Politics*, I cultivated a sense of myself as subject.[10]

Reclaiming this immersed way of knowing is part of reclaiming the commons. It's part of reclaiming our agency as subjects implicated in the larger contexts and habitats of our world. But reclaiming that agency won't come easily. It might require some affirmative action, some unlearning of deep-seated habits of deferring to experts and officially sanctioned knowledge. Reclaiming our agency also means deliberately tuning in to what we sense and notice as we immerse ourselves in a particular habitat. It means embracing what Tim Ingold calls "an original condition of engagement, of being-in-the-world."[11] In a way, it means becoming ecologically literate, or ecoliterate, although not in the way the term is generally understood today.

The term ecological literacy, or ecoliteracy is associated with educator David W. Orr and physicist Fritjof Capra who coined it in the 1990s. They wanted to bring a sense of the inherent value of the Earth and the importance of its well-being into the school system.[12] They weren't inspired by the heritage of premodern knowledge, however — almost the opposite. Their thinking was grounded in postmodern knowledge, notably systems theory and the new physics which demonstrated that energy and matter are intricately interconnected, as are time and space. Everything needs to be understood as in relationship. That's what ecology is about too. It's about the relations between organisms in a habitat, or environment. Still, it's one thing to study them and quite another to live attuned to them, and I think this is what premodern practices (immersed, dwelling in a habitat) have to contribute to our understanding of ecoliteracy: we come alive to these relationships by being immersed in them, engaged in the habitat itself. It's from these relationships that people can develop "a feeling for the organism," even a feeling for the Earth and its venerable groundwater being blasted by hydraulic fracturing (fracking) or exhausted from over-pumping.

To me, the essential thing in people, especially kids, becoming ecoliterate is creating opportunities for ongoing participation in particular local habitats. It's learning to read not just a text but the land. It's the ability to relate to the land, to read it empathetically as one would read the expression on a friend's face. It's the ability to know the soil of your garden or field through the process of relating to it over time. Ecoliteracy emerges not so much within the walls of a classroom but from prolonged participation in a habitat as living classroom. It's an apprenticeship in the traditional sense of what apprenticeships have historically involved, which is learning by doing, by attuned attention, by the head and hands working together, the senses alive to nuances of change in the living context. It's not just the sum total of knowledge (as object) that matters. It's the subject position, of implicated knowing through engagement in habitats and in situations within them, that matters.

I think of my father and what he had inscribed on a chunk of granite that's long stood at the base of that first hillside we planted with trees and which a stone mason's inscription turned into a memorial: "They cared for this land." The words are his take on what we as a family did over the years to reclaim the land as fecund. The trees we planted now tower over my head as I walk through them; they overshadow the stone with its enduring statement of what mattered to some people who inhabited this land.

15

Capacity Building #4 — Commoning Knowledge and Knowledge Commons

O NE OF MY FAVORITE PIECES OF JEWELRY IS A GOLD MEDAL-
LION my father had turned into a necklace so I could wear it,
the small gold disc nestling in the hollow of my throat. It was a medal
my great grandfather James Menzies (son of the one born at Tullicro)
was awarded by the Elma and Morningside agricultural society "for
the most number of prizes won in roots, grains and stock." The prizes
were won at its annual Fall Fair. In 1855, there were 40 county agricultural societies and 150 smaller township ones across Upper Canada.[1]
They were self-governing, self-determining, self-financing self-help organizations started by people who'd come to the Canadian colonies,
often from England, Scotland or Ireland, and taken up homesteading
in the bush.[2] The elites who ran Upper Canada weren't much interested in these people, beyond their usefulness against the threat of an
American invasion and what wheat they could supply to the export
trade. So newcomers like my ancestors relied on themselves, not just
to survive but to establish themselves and even improve their lot in
the new world. By sharing knowledge gained through direct experience
working the land of 19th-century Upper Canada and forming what I'd
call *knowledge commons* through these societies, they helped each other
and their communities develop.

The document founding the Northumberland County Agricultural Society in 1836 began: "Resolved to found a joint-stock farmers' bank of intelligence and experience upon which the agricultural population of the county might draw at liberty...."[3] During the winter, people gave talks sharing what they'd learned during the farming season, about everything from the best manuring techniques to controlling noxious weeds. Other learning took place at annual fairs (often twice a year — one in June, one in October) where people exhibited their produce and the tools and implements they'd fashioned. They also shared techniques they'd learned and answered the questions of the curious. The autumn fair was the largest, often lasting three or four days. There were prizes for crops, for breeding livestock and for the produce developed from them, such as butter and cheddar cheese. There were prizes too for the best methods of clearing land, the best ideas for rotating crops and the best implements for things like pressing cheese curd, churning butter or plowing, with a plowing match part of many Fall Fairs.[4]

In 1854, Daniel Massey exhibited a mechanical reaper that he'd invented and which he claimed could replace four men toiling through a field with handheld scythes and turkey cradles. In 1891, he and his son formed a partnership with the Harris family to found Massey-Harris, which became a multinational farm machinery corporation.[5] The wheat that Scots immigrant David Fife grew and exhibited at a Peterborough fair became known as Red Fife wheat and launched Canada's reputation as the breadbasket of the world.[6]

I first looked into all this in the 1980s when I was writing *By the Labour of Their Hands: The Story of Ontario Cheddar Cheese*. I wanted to honor the legacy of craft-scale cheddar cheese making in Ontario, at the height of which there were 2,400 often farmer-owned cheese factory cooperatives dotting the countryside, producing cheese that regularly took top prizes in international competitions, sold at a premium in London's best shops and achieved an export volume second only to timber, a major resource staple.[7] The book was also a way to write a bit of my own family's social history; my great uncle Donald Menzies was a cheese maker and, later, government cheese grader. At the time I wrote the book, I was only trying to trace the source of this industry back to what I took to be its foundations, in oral culture and craft apprenticeships, plus local knowledge and learning institutions like the agricultural societies and fairs. I didn't think to wonder where these people, my ancestors among them, had found the skills, the capacity and the confidence to found and run these institutions in the first place.

Now I look back over my research with fresh eyes. I see these initiatives as a continuity of commoning practices brought across the Atlantic on sailing ships at the time of the Clearances: the traditions of self-organization and doing things in shares, pooling knowledge and effort seamlessly, albeit adapted to the new environment. Adaptation to this new environment included learning from local Algonquin, Huron, Iroquois, Ojibwe and other tribal people still living in the areas being turned into farms. Colonists adopted some of the Aboriginal peoples' traditional clothing, such as the mukluk, their foods and herbal medicines. I imagine that the knowledge sharing would have been fairly seamless here too, with knowledge vested in stories, hands demonstrating technique and learning embedded in relationships and experience.

Honoring experiential knowledge as I did in *By the Labour of Their Hands* — and that this knowledge emerges from context (the habitat of living and working) — is a start. However, if it's to be actionable as it was for my ancestors, this knowledge needs to be gathered and shared as a knowledge commons.

Moreover, if it's to support the transformational change that reclaiming the commons requires, the integrity of the relationship between the knowledge, the implicated knowers and the habitat or context has to be honored too. And so does its dynamism, its willingness for theory to remain responsive to the complexities of living contexts, not to be rigid or static.[8] So the point is not just to gather knowledge but to ensure that the knowledge commons that we create is qualitatively different from the status quo of more corporate-identified knowledge. We can use this commoned knowledge to challenge and change the status quo itself. As John Gaventa put it in his definition of cognitive justice, the issue is "whose knowledge counts?" In the together-as-one with one another and with the land that is the ethos of the commons, everyone's knowledge counts. So does the reality of non-human inhabitants, and the habitat as a whole. To reclaim the commons as a model for how to organize and govern society, then, we must assert the legitimacy of knowledge and ways of knowing that help define that model, that bring it to life as real and actionable and just.

This doesn't mean replacing one knowledge model (objective, atemporal, static) with another. What's needed for cognitive justice is "the recognition and integration of multiple forms of knowledge and ways of knowing ... in the generation of knowledge for the purpose of social change" according to John Gaventa and Felix Bivens.[9] What's needed, then, is a model of knowledge that includes not only conventional knowledge grounded outside the lived world, but also knowledge and ways of knowing that are grounded inside it. In other words, the storied experience of participants involved in direct relations with the land, the water, the trees and with each other have an equal place as well. In a sense, a balance of literacies is required: not just the ones most at work in the built world of objects (the ability to read and write texts and to parse numbers). The literacies that parse the rhythms of life and of dialogue in community and habitat are also required. These are ecoliteracy (the ability to know a habitat through implicated participation in it) and oral literacy (the ability not just to speak but to listen and actually be affected by what the other person says, in mutually respectful dialogue).[10] As Tim Ingold wrote in *The Perception of the Environment*, "We 'feel' each other's presence through verbal discourse as a craftsperson feels, with his tools, the material on which she works; and as with the craftsperson's handling of tools, so is our handling of words sensitive to the nuances of our relationships with the felt environment."[11]

We need such an inclusive commons of knowledge both to inform and to help call forth a different vision of society from what has become dominant: one where the well-being of the habitat and the life it supports matter, not just the well-being of corporate world and the financial life it supports. Such an inclusive knowledge base would include knowledge derived from attentive, real-time participation as well as knowledge derived through objective, reductive methods. The lines of accountability — including the time lines of accountability — would flow differently as well: not just to some outside authority figure using rules of evidence to test an atemporal hypothesis about, for example, trickle-down market-economy growth (though accountability might flow through such authorities). Accountability in this model of knowing flows back to the original context and its here and now realities. It flows back to the field, to the habitat and those who are implicated in its well-being. Together with experts in, for example, soil science or ecology, all might jointly determine what must be done for the common good, what's to be done to keep a field "in good heart" or a river valley in the Canadian north today, tomorrow and for generations to come.

In Canada, the Berger Inquiry into the proposed Mackenzie Valley pipeline in the 1970s was, I think, an example of this inclusive commoning in action. A consortium of oil and gas companies, many now involved in the Alberta Oil Sands, proposed bringing development into the Canadian north through the construction of a pipeline in the Mackenzie River valley. Their feasibility studies projected the number of jobs that would be created; supplementary studies argued that the northern land-based economy supported so few people it was essentially doomed. Prime Minister Pierre Trudeau appointed Justice Thomas Berger, whose earlier legal practice had included native communities, to head an inquiry into the proposed development. Berger not only organized hearings all across the country including the north, so that the inquiry process would be open to all. He also allocated research funds to native organizations so they could bring their own knowledge to the table. One report looked at the land-based economy through the lens of the native people living there. And so, in addition to calculating the value of animal pelts sold in southern fur markets, the value of the meat from these animals that was eaten by the extended family and clan plus the furs not good enough for sale that were turned into clothing were included in considerations. In the end, Berger had essentially two sets of knowledge — both valid from their own, different points of view — to weigh and work with in making his recommendations. He also had different voices, not just those of expert consultants but those of native elders in places like Old Crow speaking of their deep and storied connection to the land. He weighed the claims of both realities and recommended a 10-year moratorium — a "stinting" in time — as the pace of appropriate development. And his recommendation was broadly accepted, as just.[12]

At the time of the Berger Inquiry, I saw the issue of inclusive knowledge and inclusive knowledge practices as justice for First Nations. Now I see it as justice for us all, all the inhabitants of Earth and the Earth itself. A society oriented to the common good and the well-being of all, not just the corporate good and the well-being of a privileged few requires it. If knowledge of what's good for all, inhabitants and habitat, is to have equal value with knowledge of what's good for a select few, the methods and practices for creating and sharing that knowledge have to be inclusively and respectfully democratic too. At least that's another important step. Moreover, it can be taken, and the capacity for this cultivated, in many settings, many social and cultural habitats. It could be in shared allotment gardens, a nonprofit organization or a community center.

An essential quality is the shift in perspective, taking seriously the point of view of being immersed in the situation, alive to relationships and interconnections. In this way we become implicated participants. Learning and knowledge flow from that attentive participation, with the senses wide open, and possibly the heart as well.

16

Capacity Building #5 — Commons Organizing and the Common Good

THE MEMORY IS 30 YEARS OLD AND HAPPILY HAUNTS ME STILL. I was attending an emergency board meeting at the cheese factory cooperative in Forfar, Leeds County, Ontario sometime in May of 1982. The meeting had been called by Talmage Stone, the cooperative president, because one of the farmer-members had died. The meeting was to start at 8 PM, but it was seeding time and the members were farmers; tending to their field work came first. Still, they all eventually showed up, most still wearing their coveralls and work boots with traces of mud on both. They gathered behind the counter in the storefront addition that had been built onto the factory itself, and settled themselves on old cheese boxes used to store and transport traditional 90-pound rounds of cheddar. They sat leaning forward, resting their forearms on their knees, their big hands hanging limp and loose between them. Talmage Stone had given hours of his time to answering my questions as I researched my book chronicling the history of cheese factories like this. "It's 90% community," he'd told me fiercely to explain how the co-op in Forfar was still in business when most other traditional craft-scale rural cheese factories had closed. I didn't know why Talmage had invited me to this meeting, but I drove out from my home in Ottawa that evening because I trusted this 84-year-old's judgment.

I too sat on a cheese box as the meeting opened with due attention to minutes from the last meeting first being received as read. Finally this retired farmer, who still sported elasticized steel bands on his shirt sleeves, broached the subject at hand. It seemed that the bylaws the members had adopted when this joint-stock farmers' cooperative was founded in the late 1800s hadn't stipulated that shares had to stay within the community or be turned back to the cooperative at the death of a shareholder. This had just always been the practice. But Talmage was worried because this practice wasn't written down as regulation. He was worried that this deceased member's share might be treated like a share on the stock market and sold to the highest bidder. "The whole company could go down the drain, one share at a time," he told his fellow board members. So he wanted to pass a resolution to block this possibility.

Gently, letting silence speak as much as their voices, the other farmers on the board of directors, all middle-aged at least themselves, pointed out that this resolution was premature. The will hadn't been read yet. The man might well have left his share to his widowed wife. And how would she feel if she learned that this had happened? I sat there watching Talmage, who'd driven the family buggy taking people to vote in the Free Trade election of 1911, who'd been reeve of the township and had fought to keep the local branch-line railway service and local school, and lost. I watched him relax as he took in the calming words and the stalwart presence of these his neighbors and his son, who'd taken over the family farm. The evening was for me a poignant lesson on the ethos of the common good and all that goes into sustaining it. A reminder too that it's always both precarious and resilient at the same time.

I use this memory now as a touchstone to conjure how it might have been for my ancestors at Tullicro as they worked out their sense of the common good and how best to pursue it. I imagine it embodying the kind of principles informing First Nations' communities, including Cree concepts like *Witaskewin*, with its notion of continuously renegotiated peaceful coexistence, and *wahakohtoin*, the unwritten code of ethics underlying relationships that work. I also imagine that my ancestors did this working out in similar everyday settings with similar plain talk, good listening, mutual respect and trust. Everyone in communities like Forfar and Tullicro was implicated in the common good, in enacting and giving concrete expression to it, and carried their share of both its benefits and its work, whether they acknowledged this or not. In Tullicro the capacity to pursue this was undermined and lost through various developments in the 17th and 18th century including enclosure of common land and denying the legitimate autonomy of local self-governing commons. In small towns like Forfar, there were less draconian developments associated with the rise of global big business, the centralization of governance and remote bureaucratic regulation.

By the time of the Clearances the common good had been reduced to the equivalent of a pauper "clothed in raiement all raggit," in the phrase of one of the clergy self-styled into "Common Wealth Men" who spoke from the pulpit and published pamphlets condemning this loss, the trend of too many self-interested people "choosing private commodity over commonwealth." (*Commodity* originally meant an advantage or benefit, not a thing.[1]) They championed "a Christian Commonwealth based on distributive justice,"[2] an echo of which can be heard in the legacy of the Cooperative Commonwealth Federation (the CCF), a strongly rural-based progressive political party founded in 1932 in Canada that, in the 1960s, united with city-based unions to become the New Democratic Party. In his 16th-century polemic *Utopia*, Thomas More deplored the insatiable covetousness ("one covetous and unsatiable cormaraunte") of the new, more commercially minded landowners creating large-scale sheep farms where "your shepe [sheep] that were wont to be so meke and tame, and so small eaters now, as I heare saye, be become so great devowerers ... that they eate up and devoure whole fields, howses and cities...".[3] In 1770, at the height of the enclosure movement in England, Oliver Goldsmith wrote in "The Deserted Village:"

> Ill fares the land, to hastening ills a prey,
> Where wealth accumulates, and men decay:[4]

This poem could have been written today, by someone in the Occupy or Idle No More Movements.

British historian and essayist Tony Judt used Goldsmith's line to title a 2010 book, *Ill Fares the Land,* in which he made this very point, interpreting the present barrenness of public virtue and the common good against the loss of it in the 18th century. "In the course of little more than a decade," Judt wrote, "the dominant paradigm of public conversation shifted to ... a view of the world best summed up by Margaret Thatcher's bot mot: ''There is no such thing as society; there are only individuals and families.'' What should be "the inherently ethical nature of public decision making" has been replaced by "a debate cast in narrow economic terms" buttressed by the "illusion" that, as Thatcher herself famously put it, "'there is no alternative,'" Judt wrote.[5]

The evidence of "decay" two centuries ago was in many commons becoming barren. The evidence today is in a similar degradation of both the social and natural environments. Socially, there are dangerously deep inequalities. More and more people are being displaced from communities and from meaningful work, with all the despair that displacement produces. In nature, the evidence is in the drying up or pollution of drinking water, the rising temperature of the ocean and atmosphere, the advent of extreme weather and climate-change refugees.

The question remains: not so much, is there an alternative, but can an alternative be articulated — not just in words but in actions and policies — so that the common good of society and of the land can be restored? Judt urged young people to get involved in reviving the state and the kind of "moral narrative" that needs to inform its policy making.[6] I agree, but also feel that this is only part of it, and that the revitalization of the state as an instrument for the common good will be a symptom of its revitalization at a grassroots, community level. I also know that many young people are already involved to the extent they can be; they are taking principled, even moral stands. What's missing, perhaps, is more at the level of capacity: the capacity to name what the common good means in the here and now and to sustain concrete actions around it. That's why I agree with Naomi Klein in urging that what she calls the "two activist solitudes" — the global and the local — be bridged.[7]

I doubt that my ancestors in Tullicro sat around making lofty abstract statements about the common good. The words of their mouths and the actions of their hands and feet were always closely aligned. They were participants in the commons, and mutually implicated in the good of the common, the very real rendering of the common good. The capacity to launch a conversation about the common good at a higher level, to shape national and even global policy making, starts here. It starts with hands, head and heart coming together with others, on the ground of real-life situations.

At least two elements of capacity building are required to revive a claim to being implicated in the common good today, and make it count for something. One is cultural while the other is more structural and organizational, although they are closely related, and both need local contexts of self-governing action in which people can participate. In one of the last things she wrote before her untimely death in 2012, Elinor Ostrom told an audience that there is no "panacea" for how to organize and run a self-governing commons. Instead, she encouraged people to think about a diversity of forms, some with governmental involvement, some with mostly private initiative, some with more community control, to fit the diversity of contexts involved.[8] The important thing to understand about the commons historically is that the binding together in mutual obligation was not imposed but chosen, again and again by daily recommitment and action by all the participants. The commons was not a collective or a commune where individual self-interest and even identity were subsumed within the collectivity, with some authority enforcing this. There was a mix of private and public, individual and shared property and responsibility, much as traditionally was the case among many Aboriginal communities. According to one Canadian account, while the territory the First Nation inhabited was considered common hunting and gathering ground, individuals and individual families were considered to "own" and possess the products of their individual labors (making snowshoes and snares, rendering meat from a hunt); they were also expected to share surpluses, with much status attached to this sharing for the common good.[9]

The important thing was the ongoing dynamic, a locally-grounded initiative of people coming together within a situation, immersed in a social and natural habitat, alive and responsive to it, and caring about it as much as their individual self-interest. From within that shared space and time, they worked together to make things, to decide things and, in the process, to sustain themselves, plus the land and local community on which they all depended. Everything was done in shares: people farmed the common infield, but with each family having their own allotted strip, much like community allotment gardens work today. People pastured their sheep and cows together at the shieling, but each family had their allotted share of that pasture in the sense that everyone observed the stinting rate limiting how many cows, sheep and goats they could send there to protect the sustainability of the common pasture.[10] People came together in work teams to share collective work such as harvesting grain and grinding it, putting in drainage, repairing roads and rock walls or dykes.

This shared effort could take the organizational form called a commons or it could as easily be a joint-stock cooperative like the Forfar Dairy, where everyone contributed a share of money as well as of milk. Commons continue to flourish in many forms in many countries of the world, including Japan, Switzerland, India, the Phillipines and the US. Fourth fifths of the upland territory in Switzerland is considered common land, its use as pasture governed by local villages and cooperatives. In Japan, some 12 million hectares of forest and uncultivated mountain meadows remained as common land until the late 19th century. Some three million hectares are still governed and used that way today, with not a single "example of a commons that suffered ecological destruction while it was still a commons," in the words of Margaret A. McKean, who's researched these extensively.[11]

Although much of the literature on contemporary commons and cooperatives treats them as economic, even business, enterprises, Ostrom's theorizing on what makes self-governing commons work stresses the linkage of the social with the ecological and the related importance of community. And that's what makes the commons an important model in building capacity for an alternative to the status quo — and could make cooperatives similarly important if their guiding principles, or ethos, are similar. Ostrom identified a number of what she initially called "design principles" and later simply "best practices" in creating sustainable commons. I detail these in Chapter 23.

There is more formality involved today, which is probably understandable because we live in a much more complex world and people often come together initially as strangers. And so, understandably, the autonomy of a local commons has to be negotiated with outside governance bodies so that its operation is congruent with larger governance principles and so that the integrity of its local self-governance will be recognized and upheld, nested within any larger circles of governance. The rules on who has access to whatever resource might be shared — water for irrigation, wood for building homes, vegetables for supper and to preserve for the winter — have to be clear. There needs to be supervision, feedback and penalties for rule breakers, just as there were field constables in my ancestors' time to ensure no one exceeded their stinting quota or otherwise broke the rules adopted for the common good. However through participation in this local socio-ecological system that works in the way living systems do, through mutual internal attunement and self-governance, people involved in a local commons invest more and more of themselves into it. They become more and more implicated in making it continue to work. Relationships grow stronger, trust deepens and so does a sense of community. The capacity to act for the common good flows from that shared community and is nested in it too, a point that's been made by many activists and commentators, including Bill McKibben in at least two of his recent books.[12] It's in small, local instances where people come together in project teams, doing things in shares, that they learn how to work together for the common good, however narrowly defined initially. In the process, they gain confidence in their own capacity to know what's going on, to contribute ideas and suggestions. As they share in decision-making and in responsibility for acting on those decisions, they gain a sense of their agency as implicated in the common good in larger circles of society. They enfranchise themselves, ready to speak up for the common good and to act on it too. And, equally important, they gain the capacity for the kind of discourse or discussion that this requires.

This is the cultural aspect of capacity building I referred to earlier, and it's as important as getting the structures right. Getting the agenda right, building consensus around genuinely common-good policies requires that the discussion itself be open, a dialogue not a debate. A debate is a contest between competing positions, based on evidence extracted from real-life situations and accountable to rules, including majority-rule votes. A dialogue, however is about relating to what the other has to say, with each speaker accountable to the habitat or context from which the storied experience emerges. There is a place for objectified evidence and expert opinion in dialogue. But in a policy forum framed to articulate an alternative vision of the common good, one that includes the good of communities and of the Earth, a dialogue that directly speaks to the urgent realities of the here and now will bring these to the fore. It might be people being displaced, or drinking water and a river habitat being compromised by oil spills or fracking in search of oil and gas. Instead of the discussion being atemporal, free floating in time as it is in a debate about the adequacy or inadequacy of, for instance, environmental regulation, it is immersed in the present, a reality demanding attention. All four of the literacies I described in Chapter 15 — textual literacy, numeracy, ecoliteracy and oral literacy — have a role in such policy discussions: two of them bringing an outsider's perspective, and two an insider's, the perspective of the embodied participant. Knowing as the capacity to relate and communicating (understood similarly as the capacity to relate to the other) are critical to dialogue. They can help to move a discussion toward consensus and genuinely trying to negotiate and reconcile differences. In fact these two literacies almost come together in what I call *civic literacy*. It's a bit like what Canadian philosopher Mark Kingwell called "political literacy" in his 2012 book of essays, *Unruly Voices*.[13] Whatever the term, it combines what public-policy thinker Robert Putnam described as "sociological WD40," a cultural lubricant essential for community[14] and what Mark Kingwell in an earlier book, *A Civil Tongue*, described as the importance of civility in public conversation. By this, he meant the importance of listening to the other person "as if they were worthy of respect and understanding" if not also with "empathy."[15] As Robert Bierstedt wrote in *Beyond the Market and the State*, power is a function of social organization in which people learn to act effectively together.[16] And that includes the ability to hear each other, not just the words but the feeling, tone and the silence that follows what is said, the silence in which a mind like that of Talmage Stone can shift.

Redirecting the governance of the global economy within the frame of the common good will take time to say the least. Cultivating the ethos of the common good so that it does inform decision-making requires ongoing capacity building which also takes time. As with meditation, there are no shortcuts because the work is experiential: participation and immersion in action situations, in shared listening, talking and decision-making around them, the articulation of policies locally and then generalizing and scaling up for more global discussions.

Global meetings associated with the World Social Forum broke useful ground in this area, and so did the Occupy Movement, with its inclusive general assemblies. These and other activist actions are enlarging the capacity for direct, participatory democracy. They're also building capacity for the kind of discussion, language and literacy that is required to genuinely articulate a common good that includes both social and natural habitats. They're not necessarily doing this instantly or perfectly. As the critiques contained in the 2007 book *World Social Forum* make clear, the habits of debating and relying on experts and celebrity cachet are hard to break. Still, the 2007 US Social Forum succeeded in framing everything in the local, and participation in locally grounded actions. One of the US organizers, Fred Azcarate (with Jobs for Justice and, later, the AFL-CIO (American Federation of Labor and Congress of Industrial Organizations)) explained that it took five years to organize the US Forum "because we wanted to do it right by building the necessary relationships among the grassroots organizations."[17] The forum was a shared open space in which local grassroots activists — implicated participants in action situations — could network, form alliances and share strategies on everything from food security to community/labor alliances to a new "taking back our cities" movement. Moreover, these implicated local activists, speaking from their experience in the community-based organizations they represented, were at the center of discussion at plenaries as well as at workshops.[18]

It's the practice that matters. I've learned this as I've found myself spending more and more time as an implicated participant in community and community building. Partly this is in the mental health community. Partly it's through a magnificently progressive church, First United in Ottawa. Partly it's through my involvement in the Gabriola Commons. There have been conflicts at the Commons, and these have been dealt with in the self-governing teams and monthly council meetings, sometimes over many meetings to ensure a healthy resolution. Staying implicated in the common good and the good of the commons and community is a big part of reclaiming the commons, though not all of it.

Capacity Building #6 — A Spirit Dialogue, Reconnecting with Creation

WHEN I WAS A KID AT THE FARM, the so-called hired man who came on Saturdays taught me to divine for water. I knew him only as Monsieur Picard, and he fascinated me, not just for his large, bulbous nose and his grey fedora hat, which he kept on his head throughout the day, no matter what work he was doing for my Dad. M. Picard also wore long winter underwear and a faded red-checked flannel shirt buttoned up to the neck during even the hottest days of summer. When I brought him fresh water from the well as he sat on the verandah eating his lunch from a black metal box, he smiled at my wondering at this, and insisted that it helped keep him cool. I don't remember why he taught me water divining, or why he chose me, and not my older sister or brother. I only remember the forked apple bough he cut for me, his big, work-callused hands engulfing mine as he showed me how to hold it just so. First, I must position my forearms close together in front of me, with the tip of the apple bough pointing straight ahead. Then I must use my wrists to apply steady outward pressure against either side of the forked apple branch. He told me to walk and keep on walking, paying attention just to the branch in my hand, its tip quivering in the fresh summer air. I walked across the horse pasture and into the maple bush toward where the old sugar shack used to stand. And suddenly I felt a tug against the skin of my fingers gripping the apple bough. The stick was turning in my hands, the tip of the bough tilting downward, pointing inexorably toward the ground. There was water. I had found water. I had tapped into a pulse, a life line of water beneath the surface of the Earth. I had made contact.

I still divine for water sometimes and cherish the opportunity to do so: choosing the apple bough carefully, speaking to the tree as I make the necessary cuts, saying a quiet *meegwetch* (thank you) then centering myself, conscious of my feet planted firmly on the ground. Then I begin to walk, and soon I feel as though I'm meditating, my wrists carrying the tautness of the tension from my arms to the arms of the apple bough. Each time the tip of the branch begins to dip, the branch turning in my hands wrapped into fists around each side of the fork, I feel a joy. I am filled with awe, and gratitude too, as I feel the connection, a connection I cannot understand, only take on faith.

I look at the stick I used last time lying on the table next to me. A divining stick. It's used to divine, which means to prophesy, to lead to the sacred, the divine. In its heyday, this stick would have been only one of many such special objects and the rituals associated with them through which people stayed connected with the sacred. I think of what Antonio Gramsci said about the role of religion and folklore in people's consciousness. In his thinking about what made it possible for people to resist deference to and compliance with the status quo of power, it was the third element, along with language and a "common sense" derived through shared experiences of labor and other social relations.[1] Before the Industrial Revolution and the advent of the six-day work week, faith permeated daily life, and nearly half the calendar consisted of holy days (from which we get the word holidays).[2] From the evidence of my ancestors at least, sung prayer and hymn were constants in daily life, a vocal tissue of sacred connection as people worked together or alone, even in tasks as simple as milking the cows. I pick up my divining stick, hold it up in front of me, then put it down. It's just a stick.

It's banal to say that a sense of the sacred has been stripped from everyday life. It's been said so many times it's taken for granted now, evoking no real sense of loss. The dynamic that disembedded the economy from the land and ways of knowing from the realms of local and bodily experience seems also to have been at work in the realm of faith. In the church tradition I was raised in, the final phase of the Protestant Reformation enshrined a remote, task-master God who judged people for their sins and rewarded them for their accomplishments. All traces of a God immanent in Creation and present in each person as well, elements that were so central to early Christianity, were gone (underground at least). The disconnect people had experienced from the land was, in a way, mirrored in the realm of faith and tradition. As the debate about whether this now-remote God does or does not exist has continued through my lifetime, the sense of disconnect has continued too. It's even deepened, though for reasons more to do with busy lives in a multitasking online world than the absence of a sense of the sacred.

Meditation has become for many people in the Western world a way to slow down and reconnect at least with themselves if not also something larger. Some of it is informed by Buddhism, with which meditation has long been associated, and some is linked to Western religions. The Franciscan theologian Richard Rohr described meditation as "prayer beyond words, prayer as a stance, prayer as an alternative consciousness."[3] The idea is not just to escape from the noise, all the trappings that guard and preoccupy the self that is alone and insecure, but to also enter the silence fully. As Richard Rohr put it, "We don't have to be smart, we just have to be present."[4]

When I meditate, I don't use a mantra to channel my way to that presence. I use my breath to get there, concentrating inwardly on the simple inhalation and exhalation of breath, knowing too that the Latin word for breathing is *spirare*, from which the English word spirit derives. Every in-and-out breath that I travel in my meditation is the breath of life, even the breath of Creation. Recalling this is at least a way to start moving toward this capacity that needs to be renewed: the ability to feel immersed in life itself, the power and presence of

Creation flowing through us, imparting the radical idea that we're not alone but connected to this larger precious whole. And implicated in it too!

It's interesting that the word salvation comes from the Latin word *salvatio*, which means "being made whole or sound."[5] In other words, argued the authors of a book about healing touch, salvation is a variation on healing.[6] Healing touch, or healing energy, has become a popular modality in therapy, practiced in secular settings (where it's often called Reiki) and in care facilities. In faith communities, where it's sometimes linked to Biblical healing stories, it's considered a way of communing with the divine.[7] Having taken the training to become a novice practitioner myself, I've begun to get a sense of how it works. It feels like an attuning of energy fields inward and outward, with my hands acting as a kind of medium, when I'm fully grounded and open to spirit energy.

Healing the disconnect within ourselves and with others is a good start. But healing also requires acknowledging the source of the disconnect and our role in perpetuating it, not just personally but in the larger world. Healing includes reconciliation. At the Iona Abbey in Scotland, some of the intentional work of reviving Celtic Christian traditions is expressed in the Iona Abbey Worship Book. It contains a "Prayer of Confession and Restoration" with the lines "….when we have not touched but trampled you in creation, when we have not met but missed you in one another…."[8]

It was in something of that restorative posture that I joined the right-relations committee at First United Church, and attended two hearings of Canada's national Truth and Reconciliation Commission, one at the Sheraton Hotel in Ottawa and the other at the Queen Elizabeth Hotel in Montreal. The commission was launched as part of the settlement in the largest class-action suit in Canadian history. Survivors from among the 150,000 Aboriginal children in Canada who, from the 1870s to the 1950s and early 1960s were placed in Indian Residential Schools and forcibly immersed in the dominant non-native culture, sought justice. The Roman Catholic and Anglican churches ran most of these schools, but the Presbyterian and United churches were involved too.[9]

I went to the hearings expecting to hear specific stories of abuse: physical abuse as the kids were strapped and sent to bed hungry just for speaking their mother tongue, and sexual abuse as well. But as I listened, it occurred to me that the larger abuse was perhaps the systemic one: the deliberate dislocation, displacement and disconnection of these children from their families, their traditions and their communities still living close to the land. The children were typically taken at age 6 or 7, and kept until aged 15 or 16, returning home only for holidays. They're called residential school survivors for a reason.

> "I have no sense of belonging, no sense of home — even in my own community," one person said. "I feel like I'm floating."
>
> Another kept her head down the whole time and spoke barely above a whisper. She began by recalling being taken away. "It was a long ride. It was a day and a night; that's how far we left our parents behind," she said. "We weren't to know that we weren't going to see our parents for a whole year.
>
> "I didn't know what love is because of what happened to me in that school. I still can't tell my children, 'I love you.'
>
> "When you put a nail in a piece of wood, and you pull the nail out, the hole is still there. And that's the way it is for me. The hole is me."[10]

As I sat there with tears streaming down my face, I wanted to only identify with that woman and sense the parallels to the dislocation my ancestors endured in the Highland Clearances. But I was on the other side of the room, the side of the colonizers. I was being challenged to identify and own up to my hand in effecting the brokenness, the dislocation, the dispossession of the people for whom Canada, not Scotland, is their ancestral home and habitat. While others got up and left the room, I stayed on in the shadows at the back. If we are to reclaim the commons, we must heal the wounds the long history of estrangement and forced estrangement have left. Equally important, we must acknowledge, challenge and resolve to change the dynamic at work behind the wounding: driving the nails in, pulling them out and leaving the holes.

There are many practices behind this that need to be named, some of which I touched on in previous chapters. In the area of faith and spiritual traditions, Christian traditions at least are rooted in a denigration of nature as no longer sacred that accompanied the doctrine of original sin and exile from Paradise. As theologian Matthew Fox wrote in *Original Blessing*, "the fall/redemption tradition considers all nature 'fallen' and does not seek God in nature."[11] Because this doctrine is associated with third- to fifth-century Christian thinkers, including Augustine and a Roman jurist called Tertullian who's credited with coining the concept of original sin[12] it's "not nearly as ancient as is the creation-centered one," Fox pointed out.[13] Still, original sin has had a devastating and lasting influence, only now being offset by new theology and scholarship. Matthew Fox himself has been a major part of this, championing what he called Creation Spirituality in a series of books. In their ground-breaking 2008 book *Saving Paradise*, theologians Rita Nakashima Brock and Rebecca Ann Parker made similar points as they recovered some of the legacy of pre-atonement Christianity. Besides water as a dominant image of the sacred, there is the tree of life. And animals abound, living in close and almost intimate relations with humans. Christ is often depicted as a shepherd at home in the fields with the sheep. He's also described as "the medicine of life." Or, rather, pursuing the path of how to live following Jesus' example is the medicine. "In sum, the early church ... taught that paradise was a place, a way of life, even an ecosystem," these authors wrote.[14] Equally, it was everyone's responsibility to achieve this, by learning to live in the state of mutually respectful affiliation and coexistence that the paradise of a healthy, balanced ecosystem requires. A lot of this learning took place before people were baptized into the church community, as an adult, and it continued through a lifelong commitment to discernment and faith judgment.

It will require a lot of capacity building to renew this sort of learning and, through it, to renew a spirit rapport, affiliation and perhaps too a spirit dialogue, with nature. I have been fortunate, even blessed, over the years in being able to observe some of the still living spirit practices of Aboriginal people in Canada, such as the women's water ceremony. I have also participated in some, including the sweat lodge, a sacred cleansing and healing ceremony that suggests reentering the womb to be reborn while simultaneously entering the womb of the Earth. And at the annual Women's Gathering in Ottawa, hosted by Minwaashin Lodge and open to all women, I've taken my turn keeping the sacred fire burning through the night and ensuring there was tobacco available for anyone coming to pray. I've leaned on these practices, opening myself to the spirit wisdom they have to teach me, and they've helped me almost learn my way back to Creation. It's as though I've renewed an umbilical cord connection with the Earth, with life on Earth, that is never meant to be cut at birth, at school or in the job market. But I've also learned how important practices and ceremonies are. Traditions and rituals are an essential medium of reconnection and reconnecting, if practiced in good faith and with integrity, over time.

When I was finally ready to leave the Truth and Reconciliation hearings in Montreal I left the building too, and went to the sacred fire that was burning in a park nearby. I knew enough to nod a greeting to the firekeepers who were tending the fire 24-7 through the four days of the Montreal hearings. Abraham Bearskin was also there. A Cree elder from Chisasibi on James Bay, he'd spoken eloquently at the hearing earlier, on a panel discussing what the "reconciliation" part of the commission's mandate might entail. It all depends on what your "ask" is, he said, what you're prepared to bring to the table and do. I knew I wanted to connect with him, but he was still standing close to the fire praying. As I waited, I thought of the minister at my church, Brian Cornelius, who would be gathering us all to board the bus back to Ottawa soon.

I recalled a line he uttered at a recent Sunday service, about the need to bridge "the chasm between our behavior and climate change." What capacities can non-native people bring to the table, not just of reconciliation with Canada's First Peoples but, through those acts and others, in the larger work of reconciliation with nature? What combination of ceremony and committed action will heal our relations with some local neighborhood, or a river that's been so abused and polluted that its water is poison even to its inhabitants? I recalled what Déline elder Morris Neyelle told me about the spirit heart that lives in Great Bear Lake. It's harder to treat a lake as merely a resource to be exploited, its water bottled for sale at the local mall, if you've begun to relate to it as a subject, even a sacred subject with a spirit heart. You can begin to consider, as Maude Barlow argued in *Blue Future*, that water has rights,[15] a claim for recognition and respect as alive and part of Creation.

As I boarded the bus, contact information for Abraham Bearskin tucked inside my journal, I remembered a song written by Pat Mayberry, a singer-songwriter friend of mine, that is included in a new United Church hymnbook called *More Voices*. The chorus, sung in a haunting waltz-beat melody includes the lines: "Called by earth and sky/ Promise of hope held high/ This is our sacred living trust...."[16] Perhaps this is what theologian Thomas Berry meant when he wrote hopefully of an emergent "ecological mode" of "cultural patterning."[17] But such a patterning won't emerge by just wishing or waiting for its emergence. It requires action, behavior-changing, consciousness-changing action at every level from the personal to the institutional and the politics of public policy.

Part III

Reclaiming the Commons — A Manifesto

An Historical Frame for Current Activism

MY WORK HERE IS ESSENTIALLY DONE. I've dug into the past to find a way of living and a way of organizing society that might be conducive to environmental balance, socially and ecologically. I've identified traditional commons practices, ways of perceiving and knowing, of doing and organizing things that might help enact this model of society. In a sense, I've also modeled what I think is the most important element, namely the commoning process itself: a process of personal reconnection and, with this, becoming implicated in the larger institutional and governmental initiatives that are needed to reclaim the commons, our shared habitats, locally and beyond.

I hope that what I've written will inspire others to embark on their own journeys, figuring out how to involve themselves in effecting changes that are necessary. In fact, I see lots of inspiring actions going on now. In this final part of *Reclaiming the Commons* I want to name some of them, particularly as I see them fitting this larger agenda. With my tongue firmly in my cheek, I'm calling this Part a *manifesto*, defined in the *Oxford English Dictionary*: "A public declaration or proclamation ... of public importance ..."[1] about what has to change.

Changes are already afoot. For much of the past 50 years, activism in North America was focused on appeals for the government to act, to defend the common good, to protect the social and the natural environment. More recently there's been a shift: grassroots movements are getting on with the necessary alternatives, taking initiatives locally and networking globally about them. Moreover, they're also often combining the personal-is-political of the women's movement, personal growth and identity politics with the more organizational and political stuff of community building and social movements. One result is that more people are consciously trying to model the alternative they're pursuing through their activism. Or, as Ghandi famously put it, they're trying to" be the change we wish to see in the world." Reclaiming the commons requires this kind of personal as well as institutional and political transformation, because reclaiming the commons also requires people becoming implicated participants inside it. This is key.

The commons is a way of doing and organizing things as implicated participants, not observers, consultants, consumers, job holders or portfolio managers. It's also a way of doing knowledge differently. Common knowledge is knowing and learning that emerges from within situations, knowing through being tuned in to working relationships and, by extension, the larger matrix of living relationships in which all life (including social and economic life) is immersed. And commoning is a way of governing and regulating society from the smallest scale to the largest in ways that are accountable to the well-being of these interrelationships and the habitats where they unfold, including of course the larger habitat of Earth. To me, these commoning practices are critical, because when I applied what I learned about them to what I've learned over my career in academia, particularly the communication theorizing of Harold Innis and Marshall McLuhan, I realized how much these practices functioned as a medium in the sense that McLuhan meant this in his famous aphorism, "The medium is the message." Commoning practices were historically the medium weaving the message of life's priorities. These practices and traditions can serve that role again, weaving a message of balance and sustainability, if they are selectively revived for use in the 21st century. They range from self-organizing and self-managing in doing things together (in shares, in teams and in work bees) to self-governing practices (for example, setting stints or limits on everything from personal and family online time to the carbon intensity of institutional activities and the pace and scale of oil and gas development).

Most importantly, the commons is a way of doing things that's embedded in the land. In fact, *the commons is a way of doing both community and economics as immersed in the here and now of living habitat.* Historically, the word common included both the common lands that had often originally been people's traditional homelands and the people who inhabited and used them. Together, land and people were an indivisible unit, an ongoing set of relationships, even right relationships if the ethos of the commons that was central to the commons culture was itself kept strong and healthy. In the historical commons, social and natural ecology were interwoven, each reinforcing the other for mutual well-being or, if things were breaking down, the opposite. Such a vision of society needs to be renewed, and can be if the practices that sustained it can be as well.

How the monopoly of our now globalized economy and its supportive thinking around the primacy of profits and free enterprise can be offset, and a meaningful shift toward thinking more attuned to the Earth and its inhabitants can be mobilized, remains very much to be seen. I see an incremental shift away from dependency on a high-strung, energy-intensive global market economy and toward a mixed model with local, self-determining autonomy nested within multiple tiers of governance and regulation. I also foresee a lot of resistence and struggle, just as what occurred when the premodern economy was displaced by the modern one.

The legacy of the commons at least offers an alternative perspective, especially for non-native people who want to work in solidarity with Indigenous activists in North America and around the world. Aboriginal people have a standing place in their still-living heritage on the land. The commons offers a similar place for others to stand outside the status quo of the global market economy. The commons heritage offers a path toward reconciliation with the living Earth and its inhabitants, human and non-human alike. The commons also offers the leverage of inclusive agency. The practice of commoning meant sharing knowledge and the act of knowing through ongoing conversations while working the fields, tending the livestock, making cheese or cloth or harvesting grain and in public meetings of the commons as well. At those meetings (called *nabec*, which means neighborliness, in Scotland), commoning meant coming together in common cause, choosing again and again to exercise self-discipline, to subdue interest in one's self and one's particular family for the good of the common, the shared well-being of the community and the land on which all depended for sustenance.

In the historical commons, everything hinged on the health of relationships, with that depending on an ethos of mutual recognition and accommodation that was at once personal and political. Reclaiming the commons, therefore, begins with, and to a large extent entails, reclaiming the skills, aptitudes and appetite for reviving the verb, to common. What this manifesto proposes, therefore, is circular. We reclaim the commons by reconstituting our capacity to common together with the land, with plants and animals and work tools and with each other. As we do this, as we recover and commit ourselves to practices of working together as implicated participants in common tasks — in community gardens and workshops or cleaning up and restoring the health of riparian lands beside rivers and streams that, left unprotected by deregulation, have become dirty and even toxic — we stake our claim to being implicated in this land and these waters. By our actions, and our confidence in taking these actions, we "enact a claim to the common," as Nicholas Blomley put it in his writing on this subject.[2] By these actions and the vision inspiring our imaginations and commitment, we help to revive long-forgotten concepts in the common sense of what's real — ideas such as what the ancient Romans called *res communi* and *res divini juris*, things that cannot be privately owned because they are meant to sustain everyone or because they are imbued with the sacred, the divine, and so trying to appropriate and exploit them for private self-interest would be unthinkable.[3]

By taking action, by engaging and participating in commoning activities, by enacting and performing a claim to the commons, we also claim or assert the legitimacy of commoning ways of thinking about and relating to the Earth and set the stage for formalizing this claim. Identifying what this vital step actually entails will come at the tipping point. It will likely involve lawsuits invoking the doctrine of public trust. It will also involve public demonstrations — even occupations perhaps — asserting the historical relevance and precedence of the premodern commons as a way to back the legitimacy of current claims to a commons. Reclaiming the commons will require a lot of organizing and sustained commitment. It will require people seeking political office and cultivating the support of existing political parties. And through it all, it will involve a constant struggle to change the language of public debate.

From the struggles of civil rights and aboriginal rights movements to women's and gay rights movements, a diversity of people have discovered the importance of language and its power to articulate what's real and important. As Naomi Klein pointed out when describing the Zapatista Indigenous land claim movement, "their true secret weapon is language."[4] Many of us have not only recovered or found our own voice. In finding it, we have reconstituted our understanding of power. We understand power now not only as something that is delegated and can as easily be gagged or cut off, but also as something inwardly claimed and asserted. It's no longer just power outside us and often in remote bastions of authority. It's power inside the situations we find ourselves in, inside the here and now, inside the habitat, the commons under threat.

In the last 50 years, a lot of personal and cultural capacity building emerged through the assertion of rights. The turn that's been occurring in more recent time is a shift from asserting *rights* toward also asserting or claiming *responsibility*. People are stepping into the gap that's being left as governments drop or merely give lip service to the common good, the health and well-being of communities and the natural environment. They are taking up the tradition of a reverse strike, which rests on people's moral right to work and to take on work that needs to be done. The phrase is associated with Danilo Dolci and the Sicilian town of Partinico where in the 1950s Dolci led a work bee in which local citizens took on some much-needed local road repairs when the government wouldn't fund them.[5] Today, I see people taking on the larger social, economic and natural environment and what road repairs are needed there. I see such self-organizing initiatives as people laying claim to their heritage as commoners, participants in the commons of the Earth, implicated in defining and defending the common good and asserting that responsibility in new and direct ways.

Perhaps you are one of these determinedly hopeful people. Perhaps you will recognize yourself in some of the details and examples in the chapters that follow. I hope so. Because it is up to us, and the choices we make personally and politically. Those who hoped that "peak oil" would force a transition to a more ecologically responsible, more sustainable economy, have been upstaged by recent developments in the fracking of gas and undersea deposits of methane hydrate. These promise, or threaten, to fuel a whole new wave of overdevelopment with devastating environmental consequences. We won't likely be rescued by circumstances. Effecting the huge and necessary changes is entirely up to us and the circumstances we create.

Every manifesto I've read focuses on collective agents of change, and names these as anonymous abstractions: the proletariat in Karl Marx's *Communist Manifesto*, the Cooperative Commonwealth Federation (CCF) in the *Regina Manifesto* and "les ouvriers" in *The FLQ Manifesto*. *The Porto Alegre Manifesto* is strangely inarticulate on the subject of agency, saying only that to make another world "[that] respects the rights for all human beings to live.... it's necessary to...."[6] These manifestos also focus exclusively on structural change and the public sphere, and ignore the private sphere where we actually inhabit our lives and ground our identity. The manifesto I'm laying out here dares to chart new ground by insisting that public and private are two sides of the same coin, that consciousness derives not just from the work we do on a job but all our actions, all our associations and the language we use to define the realities of our lives. Similarly, I see agency as both individual and collective. Mostly, I sense it being vested in relationships, in keeping with Indigenous philosophy that sees the world as a dynamic matrix of relationships seeking balance — an understanding of how life works that's been confirmed by discoveries in contemporary Western science. Agency starts with and returns to relations with the self in the here and now, and it extends outward in relations with neighbors, co-workers, friends and family, through commoning groups whether they're called by that name or by something like community garden or cooperative, school or environmental group and from there to larger forums. Agency continues through larger structures of governance and hopefully too through larger communities of more spiritual connection where a relationship with Creation and the living Earth is affirmed as well.

A commoner in the 21st century is someone who is at least cultivating the capacity for commoning at some level, from the small, local scale to the larger and probably digitally assisted scale, and from the economic to the cultural and even spiritual in scope. A commoner is an implicated participant in the common ground of everyday life as it is necessarily shared with others. As commoners, we are claiming a heritage and an agency far beyond mere spectator or consumer, job seeker or even protester. And that gives us a place to stand that is more than just resisting the status quo's take on what's real and relevant. It's a stance of persistence too: the persistence of another reality — one where living together-as-one with the Earth and honoring that connection matter at every level of existence from personal lifestyle to public policy.

This manifesto is only a sketch. What I'm sketching here is a personal and collective invitation to act, and also to imagine. It's an invitation to identify with this relic of my ancestral past, and possibly of yours too, and to explore how it can inspire you. It's an invitation to join the manifesto itself, to get involved, to immerse yourself, to become implicated in this imagining and the action that starts to seem possible by that imagining. What follows is only a sampling of such possible action linked to the amazing and inspiring wealth of all that's currently going on out there, trying to make a difference.

Where can you begin? Start where you are. Start even where it hurts: where there are gaps that you are living — materially in terms of inadequate food or shelter, economically in terms of debt or under-employment, socially as loneliness and isolation, spiritually as a longing for connection, politically as a sense of powerlessness and futility. Even taking the time to reflect on what's missing from your life is a start. It's an act of putting yourself into the picture, reclaiming your own self, occupying your own life. As I said earlier, if we want to come home to the Earth, reviving our sense of connection to it, we must first come home to ourselves, healing our relationship with ourselves and those around us.

19

Some Personal Acts of Reconnection

IT DOESN'T MATTER HOW YOU BEGIN THE JOURNEY, or whether you think of it as more personal (healing) or political. The important thing is to embrace the process of moving from being outside the changes that are needed to inside, from being an angry or indifferent bystander to an implicated participant. Start by grounding yourself and getting involved. Go for a walk, not just a power walk for exercise and to work off stress, but a leisurely hike or stroll at a pace that allows your senses to enter the passing scene. Enter further by getting to know your neighbors, your neighborhood. Join one of the *Jane's Walks* that take place all over the world, inspired by Jane Jacobs, the self-taught urban designer who wanted cities to promote connection and community. The walks started in Toronto, Canada, Jacob's adopted home town, with people leading walking tours of the neighborhoods they knew and loved. It's spread to Spain and India as well as the US.[1] The genius of Jane Jacobs, and the reason her book *The Death and Life of Great American Cities* is such a classic, is that she understood city blocks and neighborhoods as habitats: habitats that enabled, or disabled, human contact and connection.

If you live in an older inner-city neighborhood with back alleys, you could try to common that space. In Baltimore, USA, this happened in the Patterson Park neighborhood where residents got permission from the city to gate an alley. Then, with some help from Community Greens, a project of the Ashoka Foundation, they cleaned it up, installed planters and benches and created a commons for socializing and children's play.[2] For people living in apartments or condominiums, it's more of a challenge trying to cultivate opportunities for shared space and time that are handy and fit into existing patterns of life. Perhaps you have to start in the laundry room, or by posting something on the notice board by the mailboxes. The posting might pose an idea like "Let's talk about getting our kids/grandkids together, outside." Some enterprising group could start in the local park, then team up with a local environmental group (such as, in Ottawa, the Ridgewoods Outdoor Programs specifically geared to getting kids into nature)[3] and/or with a local school where teachers and parents want the kids to spend more time running freely around outside, climbing trees, exploring nature. It's important to keep coming back so that kids can really connect with a particular patch of land or riverside. In the view of Richard Louv in *Last Child in the Woods* and his work with the Children & Nature Network which he co-founded, this revisiting is crucial.[4] Only when they visit more than once do kids start paying attention, becoming curious, wanting to explore more and engage.

In Britain, the National Trust (a respected charity associated with conservation and historical sites) published a report confirming British children's disconnect from nature and have since become very involved in creating outdoor activities for kids[5] as have a number of smaller institutions, such as the Cranedale residential field studies and eco-center in Yorkshire.[6] Meanwhile, the Field Studies Council engages over 100,000 children a year through its network of residential field study centers across the country where kids get to learn about plants and animals alive and at home in their habitats.[7] More recently, Open Air Laboratories (OPAL) brought together people from the Natural History Museum and many of the country's universities, along with some lottery grant money, to create projects where kids can both learn about nature and do some citizen-science research — e.g. a twitter-based Q&A about tree health.[8]

There are no doubt similar organizations in many other countries doing similar things. Where such ventures go is an open question. Perhaps the mentors and leaders involved will encourage the kids to consider other habitats in their lives: their networks of friends online and off, their family at home, and how each is nested in the larger habitats of Earth. To me, one of the key lessons of these nature-encountering ventures is for people to start seeing themselves as participants in a living habitat, perhaps even with a stake in its well-being.

Inside North American cities and towns, Neighborhood Watch groups could combine walking the neighborhood, getting to know whose kids are whose, with some biomapping. *Biomapping* is a tool in community building, designed to put what's living there into the picture. Most maps of cities are the work of city planners and show only the official infrastructure. Biomapping harks back to premodern, survey-based maps which were more like pictures, representing space as place, as it is lived by the inhabitants. Biomapping has been used in Vancouver, Canada's Downtown Eastside to give the people who live and work on the street, including sex trade workers, a sense of presence and, with that, voice and power as residents of that place. They gained this presence through the mapping exercise as they named and marked spots in the neighborhood that are, for them, fraught with unaddressed problems.[9]

In a neighborhood where people are interested in raising some of their own food, biomapping might involve identifying possible sites for gardening — even an empty lot next to a bus stop. What became known as the "Edible Bus Stop" is an example of this. Somewhere in a working poor district of London, England, the same people who waited for the same bus every day decided to take advantage of a neglected patch of earth between some buildings and the sidewalk near the stop. They started working the soil and planting some seeds.[10] In the former East Germany, local people identified unused fruit trees on private or state-owned land and posted a digital map of their findings on a website they created. By 2012, there were 3,000 "find spots" with close to 30,000 trees which the website encouraged people to harvest, following four basic rules about fair play and responsible self-management.[11]

Another part of getting the lay of local land might involve cataloguing and checking out all the environment-related and activist NGOs and groups with an online presence as well as local members and events. In Ottawa, there are at least 50 such groups, ranging from the traditional (such as the Ottawa Field Naturalists and Ecology Ottawa) to activist groups like Friends of the Earth, relative newcomers like Sustainable Living Ottawa West (SLOWest) and Ottawa Riverkeeper. GreenOttawa.ca bills itself as the city's gateway to everything green in the area, and maintains a detailed directory of local groups and events. More inventory-making could include taking stock of local gardening knowledge, online resources such as local master gardener organizations and locally owned tools and equipment that could be shared (in suburban neighborhoods, people often share things like snowblowers to avoid the cost of every household having to buy its own). In apartment buildings and condominiums, there's less in the way of ready-made opportunity. Starting a roof-top garden or vertical wall garden takes a lot of work, though cooperation could start with sharing the work of gardening on balconies with available sun, scrounging materials for box beds or repurposing plastic pop bottles. Commoning — doing things together in shares and as a community — can start anywhere once contact is made and relationships start to form. And of course, almost anything can serve as an excuse for a potluck, potluck meals and picnics being a long-standing medium of community building. Making the meal itself together is a good ice breaker; something simple like pizzas, with store-bought frozen dough and everyone bringing their own favorite topping, is popular among younger self-organizing activists, as is a common salad bowl that can be filled in the same way.

Walking the land of your ancestors, alone or as a family project, is in a category on its own; I discovered this when I travelled to the villages and valleys in the Highlands of Scotland where my great, great grandparents were born. I wouldn't go so far as to call it a spirit quest, though it took on something of that aura as I found the particular place on this Earth where my forbears once lived in direct relations with the land — all simply by following the dry entries on a family genealogy. In walking the land they'd walked and labored and knew by heart, it's possible that I did welcome the spirits of my ancestors into my life. I was certainly amazed how much the experience meant to me, even how much it changed me. By reconnecting with my ancestors and how they lived with the land of this Earth, I found a way to connect more deeply with the land of this Earth myself. My own journey also helped me identify with the Nishiyuu Walkers: an initial group of seven young native men, led by Dr. Stanley Vollant, Quebec's first Aboriginal surgeon, who were joined by hundreds more as, in the midst of the cold and the heavy snows of February and March, 2013, they snowshoed and hiked for two months from Northern Quebec to Ottawa, Canada. Some walked to affirm life in the face of suicide, others to affirm the sacredness of the land and the waters of their homeland and others generally to embrace the goal of Dr. Vollant's *Innu Meshkenu* (Innu Road) long-walks project: Believe in yourself, have a dream, make it happen.[12] They were also fulfilling a prophecy, foretelling that in a time of disasters and crisis, young people would leave the community seeking new teachings out of which restoration will come: Mother Earth will heal and people will become one with the Earth.[13]

Leanne Simpson, a First Nations scholar and storyteller who teaches a course on Indigenous resistance at Athabasca University, commented too that these long walks (there are several going on these days across Canada) are much more than a protest, lobbying tactic or strategy. "Indigenous people," she said, "have long rallied against erasure — erasure from the land, erasure from Canadian consciousness. Putting our bodies back on the land can be very powerful." Perhaps you and a group you're part of will join one of these marches. As Simpson noted: It's "an opportunity for all Canadians to join in and walk alongside ... That's one of the ultimate goals: connection."[14]

Nor does it matter if it's healing yourself, which was the original motive of Dr. Vollant when he launched his *Innu Meshkenu* walking series, or healing relations with Canada's First Nations or healing relations with the Earth. They're all motives along the same continuum, I think. They're also part of reclaiming the commons, along with the other initiatives I've mentioned here. Putting your feet and your body (and your childrens' small feet and bodies) on the land, becoming present to others, human and non-human, in a habitat, including the neighborhood where you live, is a beginning. Reclaiming the commons begins by claiming your place within it — and in the process, awakening to a different understanding of yourself, even a different understanding of what's real and important.

Gardening, Agroecology and Forming Relationships with the Land

CLAIMING OR RECLAIMING A CONNECTION TO THE EARTH requires more than occasional walks in the country, however. Like doing meditation or some other practice that helps you reconnect with yourself, the activity must be ongoing. It must also, I think, be intentionally linked to changing the microenvironment in which you dwell, the microhabitat of time and space in which you live. So if you ask yourself "How green is my life? How green is our home?" you are asking larger questions. Since at least the time of William Shakespeare in the English-speaking world, green and the forest have stood in symbolic counterpoint to the power politics of cities and empires. Greening in this larger sense doesn't mean the creation of "green jobs" in, for instance, the wind power industry, although that can be a byproduct.

Thinking along these more traditional lines, greening means embracing an ethos of coexistence, even right relations, *within* habitat rather than mastery *over* it. It means cultivating the power to relate, not just to control. Acting on this, contributing even to a commons consciousness, means cultivating a relationship with the Earth, coming to know it through that connection. This might involve something as simple as gardening, or engaging in a reforestation project such as what I was part of as a kid or the kind associated with the Landcare scheme in

Australia.[1] It might involve forming or joining a group to tackle the cleanup of a local pond, lake or river, as happened around the Don River in Toronto and the Hudson River in New York. The Canadian project was launched in 1969 with a mock funeral for that lethally polluted waterway by an uppity group called Pollution Probe. Forty years later, despite most of the usual messy setbacks of trying to make real change, there are salmon swimming upstream again. Twenty wetlands have been restored, 600 hectares of land have become public domain and thousands of trees and flowers have been planted.[2] A similar citizen-led cleanup of the seriously sick Hudson River in New York State led to the formation of the Riverkeeper, which has taken this dream of common cause, common good river reclamation and the policy activism around it elsewhere,[3] with some considerable celebrity support from Robert Kennedy Jr.

Gardening might be the most accessible activity for most people, because it can be done on a larger, group or neighborhood scale but also, at least at first, with containers on an apartment balcony. Whatever the scale involved, gardening doesn't just involve but requires an ongoing relationship with soil, with plants as they emerge and grow tall or wide and with bugs, figuring out which ones are friendly and which are not. The experience, the living out of relationships with everything in the garden, grounds you in time as life, continuity and life cycles. True to how I defined ecoliteracy in Chapter 14, gardening also requires paying close attention from within the relationships you've entered in the habitat. It involves learning by observation and improvising, though also where appropriate, turning to outside authorities to do some research. If you're in a community or allotment garden, it will probably involve getting to know your neighbors, swapping observations, sharing hunches and theories.

This isn't the place to talk about how gardening is being used as a medium for healing for people recovering from addiction and mental illness. (It's called variously "green therapy" or "horticultural therapy" in these settings).[4] Still, it's worth knowing because this signifies how important gardening is for mental health. Grounded connection with a living habitat, however small, is part of what it has traditionally meant to be human.

School gardens have taken off in many countries as a way to get kids in touch with the natural world and to engage them in growing things so they know where food comes from. One of my favorites is a ten-minute walk down the road from Tullicro, the commons fermtoun in the Highlands of Scotland where my great, great grandfather was born in 1792. Called the Breadalbane Academy Community Garden, it's a collaboration between the local high school, scout group and older local citizens on an expanse of donated farmland along a country road outside Aberfeldy, where the school is located. It's a lovely, food-rich place alive too with birdsong, or it was when I wandered through it on a misty September day. There are pear and apple trees, black currant bushes, several vegetable beds and at least one herb garden, plus nicely tended pathways among them, a picnic bench in one nook and a bench for just sitting on a piece of high ground. The children can earn a "rural skills" credit through their involvement in the garden, and the school won an award for its programming in this area.[5] In Canada, what had been a trash-filled courtyard at the Windemere Secondary School in Vancouver was transformed into a garden with 13 plant beds, a greenhouse and an acquaponics system filled with plants and fish where Grade 10 Science students study the nitrogen cycle at work in a mini nutrient recycling system.[6] Also in Vancouver, the UBC Farm, occupying 24 prime hectares on the university's south campus, is home to a Children's Learning Garden with raised beds, a greenhouse and also an adobe oven and small teaching shelters.[7] An Ottawa-based charity, Nutrients for Life, supports what has emerged as a school gardening network.[8] Community gardens, allotment gardens, locavore food farms are all on the rise too, as people seek food security through local sourcing and an alternative to food that's burdened with pesticides and herbicides. Books like Dickson Despommier's *The Vertical Farm: Feeding the World in the 21st Century* attest to the innovative use of space in dense urban settings, with both rooftop greenhouses and vertical ones being installed in various public venues.[9] In 2011, Toronto, Canada became the first North American city to adopt a bylaw requiring all new buildings of a certain size to have a roof capable of supporting roof-top gardening and green-houses.[10] Many of these initiatives are commercial, but they can also be sponsored by community groups, NGOs, schools working with community centers, faith groups, even seniors' centers; they can use the commons or the cooperative as an organizational model as well (see Chapter 23).

Detroit, USA is an interesting case. During the late 1990s and early years of this century, a combination of deindustrialization and financial crisis resulted in a third of city properties being abandoned. Ad hoc gardens sprung up on these abandoned lots, and as relationships grew up around them, organizations and associations grew as well. By 2009, the local urban farming network included 700 community gardens. One example is at Romanowski Park in Southwest Detroit. Here, local public schools collaborated with a group called Greening of Detroit, Michigan State University Extension, a soup kitchen run by the local Capuchin Monks and American Indian Health and Family Services to run a minifarm/garden project that both supplies local fresh food and also educates youth and the local community in sustainable ag-ricultural practices. Greening of Detroit now supports some 1,400 food-producing projects throughout the city.[11]

In Toronto, Canada, some downtown community gardening emerged from a different source, a food bank operating from the community center at Symington Place, a public housing project in one of the city's poorest and least serviced neighborhoods. It started with Nick Saul, the food bank's newly hired executive director, tellingly with a background in community organizing and political activism and with a personal distaste for food banks as a mere Band-Aid™ on distress. What has become celebrated internationally as The Stop now calls itself a Community Food Center, which uses access to healthy food and the power of this healthy food to transform lives and the community. In addition to still operating a traditional food bank, the Community Food Center also has a large garden outside, communal dining and cooking programs, a weekly health and nutrition group for low-income pregnant women, breakfast and lunch drop-ins and projects promoting civic engagement. The center also has a satellite location, the transformed site of one of the city's major transit-vehicle maintenance buildings, now called the Green Barn. It is home to a weekly farmers' market, sustainable food education programs for kids, a greenhouse, outdoor gardens and a food enterprise, catering and hosting fundraising dinners in, for instance, the greenhouse.[12]

In Halifax, Canada, an initiative called the Common Roots Urban Farm is actually located on an historical Common, the Halifax Common, which was created in 1763 by King George III of England. Originally 235 acres, only 20% of which is still open to the public today, this common was meant "for the use of the inhabitants of Halifax forever."[13] The land devoted to this urban farming commons is officially under the control of the Capital District Health Authority, which puts this initiative interestingly under the rubric of health and healing. The Common Roots website posts an "engagement menu," offering escalating levels of participation, from "light farming" which involves attending gardening workshops and dropping in for a chance to get your hands dirty a bit, to "medium farming," which involves showing up for the weekly work bees or bringing school groups to "full season farming," which might involve renting a plot for the season.[14]

All of these gardening activities give people a chance to move beyond just connecting with the Earth. It's a chance to cross the threshold, to make the transition from being an outsider to an insider. As people garden, they're entering a relationship with a local habitat — plants, soil, water, compost and, yes, worms and earwigs and other insects too. Being conscious of this, and consciously cultivating this sense of intentional engagement and immersion in living relationships is key. It's the hinge that turns the activity into more than just getting a bit of outdoor exercise and growing a bit of your own food. You become a participant in a habitat, even co-creating it through the work you do. In the process, you can become implicated in its well-being, not just getting to know if it's "in good heart," but starting to care as well.

In fact, gardening is hard work, stretched out over several months of the year. Many people abandon city allotment gardens, or don't continue after a first excited year because they don't have the time or the patience for sustained commitment, or perhaps they've grown used to the instant results of potted plants from a garden center. So there's merit in considering gardening as a group effort, especially when viewed through the larger lens of commoning and reconnecting with the Earth. This might involve becoming a volunteer at a school garden. Or getting your fitness or running group to take on an allotment garden as a collectivity. A book club could decide to garden together as well, if not in one member's backyard, then in a local allotment, inviting a local master gardener to one of their winter meetings, perusing the pages of a venerable seed-house catalogue. A local faith or social justice group could take on the task of turning a local food bank into a community food center, tapping into the downloadable advice and shared knowledge available at Community Food Centres Canada's website, an organization Nick Saul created to spread this concept.

Group settings are more conducive to discussion, so that sharing the work extends into sharing new knowledge and learning. Some of this might involve, especially among children, affirming the ecoliteracy to be gained as people use all their senses while they handle young plants, and work their fingers through dirt or compost. Becoming eco-literate doesn't just mean learning about the relationships between living things in an ecosystem from outside them, in textbooks. It means coming alive to them from within that webwork of relationships as you yourself become a part of them, attentive to them and even attuned to their realities. It means developing a feel for the environment from being immersed in it and in the process, perhaps too coming to care, to respect the complexities involved and maybe even feel joyful as you witness the effect of your actions. You can then bring that insider's perspective, and empathy, to larger discussions about climate change and toxins in the water as well as more local ones, such as Food Secure Canada's People's Food Policy for Canada, the goal of which is to shift food policy from "market-driven global supply chains to a more complex, regenerative, social and ecological web of relations."[15] Not that a few local gardens are going to make much difference. But they can if they're seen by participants as part of a larger vision of change, and if implication in this local action can inspire implication in what's needed to bring larger changes about.

Meanwhile, permaculture and agroecology take the notion of growing food in a way that relates to and works with habitat to a larger scale. Permaculture emerged in the 1970s in response to the rising cost of farming and also what modern agribusiness was doing to the biosphere. In a master's thesis on permaculture, Carleton University graduate student Chris Bisson summarized permaculture's core principles:

1) care of the Earth
2) care of people
3) fair share
4) setting limits to population and consumption

Bisson described permaculture as "an ethics-based design process" that intentionally mimics how nature works, interdependently in a matrix of mutual relationships.[16] Agroecology involves working with habitat and within the limits of its carrying capacity, for sustainability. In *Agroecology: The Ecology of Sustainable Food Systems*, pioneering agroecologist Stephen R. Gliessman defined agroecology as focused on whole systems and dynamic equilibrium, and roots its approach in the classic understanding of ecosystems, which are all about "complementary relations between living organisms and their environment." Gliessman also defined agroecology as both a field of study and a "change agent" to help shift agriculture to a "truly sustainable basis."[17]

There is evidence that this change is moving ahead. A UN study of agricultural practices in 57 countries found that eco-farming had increased average crop yields by about 80%, adding that "agro-ecological methods outperform the use of chemical fertilizers in boosting food production where the hungry live — especially in unfavourable environments."[18] In the US, university extension departments are working in partnership with farmers interested in habitat conservation and ecologically responsible farming practices. They're building on often multi-generational connections to the land that, in its expression as resistence to the Keystone XL Pipeline cutting through Nebraska, has been described, by one observer at least, as even stronger than among some environmentalists.[19] Washington State University researchers have developed participatory breeding programs in which they collaborate with farmers to develop and test locally relevant, low-input varieties of seeds and livestock.[20] There are many bottlenecks, including agroecological farmers gaining access to the big grocery chains in the mainstream, which speaks to a deep divide in North American food production: most is concentrated in the hands of huge agribusinesses. In the US, the top 2% of family and corporate farms generated 59% of sales. The largest 10% of farmers also collected 74% of government produce subsidies and supports.[21] Still, alliances are being formed facilitating scale-up. New food assembly and distribution hubs are being created for farmers producing on a larger scale but still using more responsible agroecological practices.[22]

An Economy of Fair Trade
and Right Relations

THAT GARMENT WORKERS IN BANGLADESH CONTINUE TO BE KILLED as the unsafe buildings where they work collapse or burn[1] and Amazon rainforests continue to be destroyed to make way for cheap beef farming brings home the cruel tyranny of the profit margin that drives the global stock market which in turn drives production to the lowest possible input cost wherever, whenever and however possible. Resisting this paradigm requires action on many levels, including the personal: we can refuse to be complicit in sustaining such situations. We can also become implicated in institutionalizing alternatives including fair trade. Fair trade, like fair labor, is based on the traditional values of mutual recognition and respect, or right relations, values that informed the regulation of markets in the premodern era.

The campaign to "make trade fair" is sometimes associated with Oxfam, which was already involved in bringing justice to international development when world coffee prices plummeted by 50% between 1999 and 2002, squeezing the bulk of the world's 25 million coffee producers, most of them small farmers with small landholdings, into debt and bankruptcy. Oxfam launched its fair trade campaign in 2002 by lobbying the biggest coffee companies, including Kraft and Nestle, to pay a fair and living wage to coffee producers. Oxfam didn't get very far until they switched focus; they started to engage coffee drinkers in local actions. The idea behind this new campaign was to help consumers see their connection to the people who produced their coffee and urge them to recognize their responsibility to respect what the farmers were asking: fair compensation for their work in growing coffee. And the campaign worked. People weren't just buying coffee anymore. They were buying into a relationship with coffee farmers, some of whose pictures they got a chance to see, some of whose stories they got a chance to learn about.[2]

Such fair trade campaigns represent a small step toward renewing the ethos of the market that prevailed when the premodern economy was embedded in the social relations of a local habitat or community. A lot of people think that this economy was purely subsistence, but in fact there was a lot of trade, and this included local markets where people sold surpluses and bought what they needed and wanted. The market, however, wasn't run by supply and demand. It was run by customary laws, rules and protocols grounded in the local common good. A reasonable price for essentials like flour and oats was set when the market opened, with initial business restricted to direct users. This meant that people's needs were met first, and would-be hoarders and price gougers were kept in check.[3] Although the term *right relations* wasn't part of the vocabulary of that place and time, this was the ethos on which trade was conducted. And it can be again.

It seems almost frivolous to mention the computer app to support what is called a *buycott*. People can scan the bar code of an item in a store, and the software will signify whether the company making and selling it has been flagged for unfair or unsafe working conditions.[4] Still, for the time-squeezed, this at least is a step toward becoming more responsible and implicated. It's a step away from the indifferent calculus of the market economy. At least potentially too, it's a step toward solidarity and the mutuality of a more commons-inspired alternative. Mutuality is critical, because it involves mutual recognition of the other in an economic relationship. As identification deepens, this can extend to include not only humans and non-humans but the other of the habitat too. An example that might initially seem esoteric: two Palestinian brothers now run a Halal slaughterhouse outside of Ottawa called Mr. Beef. In the Halal tradition, what might be called right relations doesn't just apply to the moment of slaughter, which is to be done mercifully and with respect for the animal sacrificing its life. Rights relations include treating the animals well from the moment they arrive in the pens where they are fed a last meal or two. The brothers also source animals from local farms where they have been assured the animals are cared for well. Imagine renewing right relations with the soil, with the water in local rivers and lakes. I think of that phrase used by premodern commoners, a field maintained "in good heart" through responsible care and use of it, and of an Aboriginal elder telling me about a heart in the middle of Great Bear Lake, the water heart. It will take a lot of consciousness raising to revive such deep mutual sensibility, and a lot of change in policies, in institutions and in behavior in the here and now.

There's at least some preliminary shifting happening. Many local food box programs, in which people contract to receive a box of fresh vegetables through the growing season, also include an invitation to drop by and, sometimes, to get involved. Juniper Farms in the rolling hills of Western Quebec outside Ottawa, Canada invites the families who contract for a share of the vegetables to come regularly and bring their children. This way young people can get their hands in the dirt, learn how food grows and form at least the beginnings of a relationship with those who grow food for them. In the US, community supported agriculture (CSA) can involve a standard box of vegetables, though increasingly boxes may also include eggs, herbs, flowers and sometimes meat. In 2009, a Local Harvest survey showed 2,877 farms were involved in CSA programs across 50 states. A 2012 study put the number at 3,637, and calculated that this food was likely reaching 180,000 households and feeding one million people.[5]

As well, farmers markets have been growing at about 5% annually since the late 1990s in the US, faster than CSAs, and their effect can be transformative.[6] When I spend time at the ones around Ottawa, I see people going to the same stalls week after week; I see rapport starting to develop. Buying and selling is still a transactional relationship, but there's some mutual recognition happening, and the beginnings of re-spect out of which paying what's fair to the grower makes palpable sense. For many, buying at a farmers' market or signing up for a weekly food box might start as a lifestyle choice or even riding the bandwagon of the latest trend. Such implicated initiatives can at least foster faith that another reality is possible and that personal, local choices and actions are part of helping a new food system to emerge. Still, organizational infrastruc-tures and public policy support are needed to take this vision to the next level, and this is where one of the biggest challenges lies. Right now, the choice that most people perceive is still between an essentially com-mercial model, or a government- or non-governmental service-delivery agency, like those associated with a Community Food Center or Food Bank, with paid staff offering food programs and volunteers and clients assisting, or ad hoc grassroots initiatives run on desperate or idealistic volunteerism, often responding to crisis situations, such as the urban farming that emerged in the inner city of Detroit. A lot of self-organizing, self-help food sourcing initiatives also emerged in Detroit in the 1930s, also on abandoned private property; yet little of this continued beyond the moment of Depression-era crisis to become the basis of a commu-nity economy. Community building, the knowledge, the associations and the ad hoc self-governing infrastructure disappeared completely. And these disappearances might happen again as, for example, Hantz Farm Detroit, billing itself as the world's largest urban farm, sets itself up as a commercial operation in the city, reasserting the business model as the taken-for-granted norm of how best to get things done.[7]

Yet a more commons-inspired and community-based model is a viable third alternative, and it seems to be increasingly seen as such. Some, like the Gabriola example I described in Chapter 11, are ac-tually called commons. In Kamloops, BC, the Kamloops Food Policy Council started a public garden on land donated by citizens, and in 2013 the city followed suit with two more gardens, including a raised bed at City Hall featuring strawberries and pumpkins. In Baltimore, USA, local master gardeners have volunteered to tend a patch of col-lards and chard in front of City Hall, with the greens sent to the local food bank. In Seattle, enough food was grown on public parkland in 2010 to provide nearly 42,000 servings to nonprofit agencies in the area. The city's Public Utilities office has since opened the Beacon Hill Forest where the public can forage for berries, nuts and fruits.[8]

In a Toronto, Canada *Globe and Mail* feature summarizing some of these "public produce" initiatives, Sarah Elton, author of the bestselling book *Locavore*, wrote that this "recalls the 'commons' that people who lived in rural communities shared" for growing their food.[9] And it seems to me that most if not all of these initiatives could be run within a commons frame of governance: organized, directed and controlled by local community participants. In Chile, independent fishers organize themselves into self-managing fisheries under common "territorial use rights in fisheries" (TURFs), with their commons organization taking a physical presence merely as a pier, a boatyard and huts which the fishers share (sharing the upkeep as well).[10] In the deindustrialized city of Holyoke in Western Massachusetts, USA, a nonprofit community organization called Nuestras Raices (Our Roots) is the hub of an expanding set of community initiatives that has actually been dubbed an "urban commons." Beginning in 1993, Nuestras Raices began converting empty lots scattered through downtown Holyoke into what is now a network of nine community gardens. Consciously drawing on the largely Puerto Rican local people's knowledge, which for many included farming, they set out to achieve local food security, to give young people a chance to learn skills and to stay off the streets. Over 100 families grow food in the garden plots, each plot generating up to $1,000 worth of food to offset poverty-line family budgets. Young people have been taught marketing skills and now sell garden produce at a local farmers' market. Nuestras Raices bought an abandoned building from the city and turned it into a multipurpose community center where people learn nutrition and commercial food preparation. There's also a greenhouse, a business incubator, a commercial kitchen and a restaurant where local foods are served, along with bread from a brick-oven bakery in the incubator.[11]

A project doesn't have to be called a commons, however. It could be a cooperative, an organization with its roots in the same locally

grounded ethos of shared responsibility and obligation for shared benefit. In Manitoba, Canada, there is an association of farmers' markets,
organized as a cooperative[12] In Haiti, it's called *konbit*, following Afro-
Caribbean tradition associated with mutual assistance and cooperative
work. A Haitian organization called Le Centre Haitien du Leadership
et de l'Excellence (CHLE) is supporting a revival of konbit in local, citizen-led development projects. It's pulling together the private sector,
national and international NGOs, political parties, Haitian government
agencies, universities and grassroots groups to back and facilitate them.
A report on this initiative, co-published with the Coady International
Institute based in Nova Scotia, Canada, which is one of the supportive
NGOs involved, recounted several examples. One, a women's collective called *Kodinasyon Fanm Rivye Kano* or KOFAR, emerged from a
general assembly of the women of a rural area called Saut d'Eau where
women decided to pool their savings and work together, adopting an
informal charter of principles, including accountability, transparency
and personal financial investment. Their first member-funded project
involved collecting fruit that arrived at local markets overripe or crushed
and turning this into confitures and cream liqueurs. In a second project,
the women established a community garden to grow their own fruit for
what had turned into a burgeoning fruit-product business. Every new
KOFAR project is designed by members and approved by vote before
outside financial partners are sought out. Seven years later, and continuing on a project-by-project basis, the women's self-help collective
has created a $20,000 food processing facility and cultural center that's
used for many community events, including around family planning,
women's health and nutrition, environmental protection and fundrais-
ers for more projects. In another rural project, farmer-residents of Bailly
formed an organization called *Inyon Gwoupman Peyizan Bay* (IGPB)
within which small groups or teams of 8–15 people self-organize to
take on various common-good tasks such as constructing stone walls,
planting trees, preparing compost and clearing fields, while the larger
collective looks after things like developing a seed bank for members'
use. A third project emerged in Cite Soleil, best known up to that point

as "the most notorious slum in the Western Hemisphere." It started when a young resident, Stephen Italien, got fed up with how the runoff from heavy rains swept other people's garbage into his street and the canal that ran through the neighborhood. He rallied some neighbors and together they gutted old television sets and used the casings as garbage cans. After another group spontaneously copied this and cleaned up another city block and then another, a group of 20 young women and men got together and founded *Soley Leve* (Rising Sun). They wanted to continue the momentum, using the same shared leadership, loose self-organization and cooperative effort to clean more streets, plant flowers, install street lights, paint boats and organize festivals, and using everything from megaphones and flyers to Facebook and blogs to spread news of a new initiative. The group has eschewed a formal organizational structure with office, board of directors, formal program. As one founder said "... we are about the spirit of *konbit*." And another, striking a slightly more practical note, added: "Social movements don't need a lot of money, they just need a visible result."[13] In other words, there's virtue in staying grounded in the here and now, working with what's available in the here and now to make a small change in the here and now, inspiring participants that they can make a difference.

What matters is the implicated participation. What matters too is mutuality, coming together in mutual obligation and self-interest as a neighborhood or community if not also around the shared use and habitation of some land, as was the case with my ancestors on the premodern Commons. This participation is what the legacy of the commons and other commons-like organizing has to offer. It involves leadership from within, specifically from within relations of shared work and other resources, including money, being vested in an enterprise. It involves right relations, shared responsibility and accountability. It also requires supportive structures that, as in the premodern commons, are more flexible and vested in principles and customs rather than rigid and bureaucratic; this keeps mutuality alive and fresh.

Such self-organizing and self-governing on a team scale and project scale can be used in running small projects nested within larger structures of, for example, a community center, community food center or even a shopping mall. The capacity for commoning that participants develop in the process can then be taken elsewhere, perhaps into a spin-off enterprise organized as a local cooperative, as happened with the Community Kitchen at the Gabriola Commons in BC. In Toronto, the Toronto Community Housing Corporation (TCHC), one of the largest housing providers in North America with 164,000 tenants and 1,542 staff, decided to import the participatory budget-planning model used so successfully to mobilize responsible citizen participation in Porto Alegre in Brazil. Twenty-seven elected tenant representatives sit on a tenant council deciding priorities for allocating the $10 million yearly capital fund of the corporation. Plus, tenants themselves can make proposals, at an all-day meeting that all tenants can attend. The sense of confidence in making a difference has subsequently spilled over into electoral politics, with "TCHC tenants mobilizing across the city 'with an amazing ability to communicate among themselves.'"[14]

Also in the public sector in Canada, the Canadian Federation of Students (CFS) has developed an Ethical Purchasing Network through which it sources student t-shirts, tote bags etc. in partnerships with, for example, a cooperative called the Single Mothers of El Salvador.' [15] In Manitoba, the University of Winnipeg's food services division has been reconfigured as a "self-governing" social enterprise called Diversity Social Enterprise Initiative, with "participatory management where decisions are made in collaboration with the workers," at least according to their vision statement.[16] It sources food for its cafeteria from local farmers and even herbs from an on-site garden plot tended by the staff and has established direct relations with fair trade sources of coffee, tea and sugar in the global south. In British Columbia, the UBC Farm has a lot more scope for shared action and governance since it includes both a working farm, a twice-weekly farmers' market and extensive integration of learning with a rich array of activities, including those associated with and honoring the Musqueam people on whose ancestral lands the university stands. And the spirit of participatory teams and local self-governance is strong, dating back to the late 1990s when it was students who led the effort to revitalize the farm and save the land from being turned into housing. Today, the UBC Farm is formally part of the Faculty of Land and Food Systems. Still, "I would say that we do have a lot of room for self-governing," Amy Frye, director of the Centre for Sustainable Food Systems at UBC Farm, wrote to me in an e-mail. "We have a long history of staff-led innovation and we continue to be pretty self-governing/managing on the ground ... We are very self-organized with regards to our staff and team members."[17]

This spirit of do-it-yourself (DIY) self-organizing is re-invigorating the labour movement, giving rise to more spontaneous actions, such as single-day strikes and 'Fairness' campaigns. According to Nora Loreto, a Quebec-based writer, musician, activist and editor with the Canadian Association of Labour Media, restoring a sense of shared community is a big part of this new organizing, as is taking the initiative in creating worker co-ops.' [18]

Cooperatives, at least in theory, belong to an alternative model of economy, one that, like the premodern economy, is grounded in the community if not also the local habitat and relations of mutuality among citizen-members. Traditionally, like the Forfar Dairy I mentioned in Chapter 16, co-ops are financed by participant shares; they're self-governing and embody an ethos of the common good. An estimated one billion people belong to cooperatives worldwide: housing cooperatives, work and business cooperatives, including some still-operating dairy cooperatives in Canada. In 2008, the largest 300 had a combined annual turnover of $1.6 trillion. In India, 67% of rural households' food and related needs are supplied by agricultural cooperatives. Forty per cent of African households belong to a cooperative. And in Canada, there are 9,000 cooperatives, including financial institutions like the Desjardins Caisse Populaire, with 18 million members and approximately $50 million in annual revenues.[19] Together, these institutions could become part of an alternative economy, or at least a substantial sector within a more diversified world economy than we have at the moment. Cooperatives, like the community, sometimes called "customary," economy of premodern times, are not run on the profit motive. Their purpose is not to make profit, and as much of it as possible. Their purpose is sustaining life: the life and livelihood of participants and the shared habitats, social if not also natural, that support this. A modest return on investment is sufficient for this purpose, a return geared to the carrying capacity of the habitats involved, and also their need for sustainability.

There's no reason why this other economic model, or these other different sectors of a more diverse global economy can't gain ground, especially as Internet connections allow for direct sourcing of materials and food from like-minded enterprises around the world. I think of the worker cooperatives in South America behind the production of my favorite chocolate bar or coffee, and the networked connections that bring us together in fair trade transactions. What's needed is leadership, but the right leadership: leadership from within the groups and organizations whose vision is to change and heal the world; leadership traditionally associated with the democratic, self-governing commons. In Berlin, Germany, there's actually a commons-promoting office within the city's administration. Called Allmende-Kontor, it has helped local people reclaim the site of the Berlin-Tempelhof airport as a community garden, with raised beds covering some 5,000 square meters of land and ad hoc gardening happening in discarded bed frames, baby carriages and bathtubs. As a local sociologist, Christa Muller noted: "no grand new societal utopia is being promoted. Instead, simple social interactions slowly transform a concrete space in the here and now, building an alternative to the dominant order based on market fundamentalism."[20]

There's nothing stopping a bunch of activist groups, involved in a range of social and environmental justice causes from coming together with the same idea in any city or town, to start commoning. A local community IT network could also take this on. Interested representatives from different groups could form a team, reach out to learn from others (e.g. the Gabriola Commons, the International Association for the Study of the Commons, as well as organizations specializing in promoting community development and citizen-led initiatives) and introduce commoning principles and practices in joint-action local projects, including in the area of local food security. Such common cause projects can at the same time tackle the global and local activist divide, bringing members of national and international groups together with local, grounded activists. Through real-life actions they collectively pursue in the local habitat, they'll not only inspire participants with proof that their efforts can make a difference. The experience might also gently remind them of the time and effort that's involved. The collaborative, intergroup process itself could be an act of commoning, starting to cultivate a commons in the local community with its own common knowledge and consensus on what's important.

Common Knowledge and
Knowledge Commons

IN THEIR BOLD AND SASSY BOOK *A POSTCAPITALIST POLITICS*, two feminist academics who publish under the combined name of J.K. Gibson-Graham champion the revival of agency, especially in the realm of knowing and naming what's real. They champion being a beginner, daring to not know and being open to new learning from direct observation, attentive experience. They advocate the practice of *weak theorizing*, coming up with tentative, small ideas rather than big, master-narrative theories. They quote a Zen master, Shunryu Suzuki, who noted that "In the beginner's mind there are many possibilities, in the expert's mind there are few."[1]

Inclusive knowing and knowledge creation can help change status quo realities; I know this because I am a recovering expert. As I mentioned earlier in this book, I traded in the credentialed authority to speak for others (using existing data, master theories and scaled-up statistical analysis), along with a cozy and lucrative place on the conference circuit speaking as an expert. I gave up speaking through assigned frames of what was real — or what Dorothy Smith, a sociologist of knowledge, has called "the conceptual practices of power"[2] Instead, I found the courage to speak for myself, and only for myself. Equally important, I also found the patience to listen to others as they embraced what they knew on their own terms, so that, together, we could work toward our own shared sense of what was real and important.

There are many ways in which knowing relates to change, but I will focus on only two. The first of these is what I call *commoning knowledge*. This is knowledge gleaned in common by insiders as insiders, participants alive to an action or situation in which they're involved, and accountable to it too. It's what I referred to earlier as knowledge arising from connection and relationships of implicated participation versus more remote, objectified knowledge associated with texts and data, and accountable to outside authorities. Such common knowledge is often knowledge associated with so-called amateurs such as master gardeners. Ottawa master gardener Tom Marcantonio describes this knowing as "deep, internalized knowledge and intuition."[3] It is knowing that emerges almost out of the ground, the ground of experience, rather than from theory. But it is a valid way of creating reliable knowledge and, if it's honored, can lead to new policy, even if only initially at a local level. Meanwhile, commoning knowledge enfranchises locally engaged people as knowledgeable participants who have something to say out of their direct and even respectful relations with the soil, the land, the habitat. It affirms them as change agents, with their attentive immersion in the habitat helping to substantiate a claim to be part of that change. As these participants get a chance to bring their knowledge and their sense of what's real and important to various tables of discussion, they bring with it a sense of the local habitat with its own agency, its own claim for recognition, through the perspective of their relationships within it. And that can make a difference, helping to nurture what I've been calling the *ethos of the commons*, a feeling for, if not a fully together-as-one connection with, the Earth, through shared engagement with it.

A lot of this kind of knowing and learning is happening under labels like "experiential learning" and "learning through play" (among children) and, among adults, "peer-to-peer learning," "social learning," "participatory knowledge," "participatory evaluation" and sometimes "citizen science." OPAL has invited kids from across the UK to participate in surveys trying to map the health of everything from local soil and water to air and local trees. On the OPAL website, there is a pond health survey map, where the results of local pond water tests that kids, under supervision, have done are posted.[4] Downloadable instructions and apps, combined with local scientists and science teachers, could take this idea further, not only yielding useful information on whether local fields and ponds are "in good heart." If the testing and data gathering are done with mindful intent, this can also help to affirm the more psychological, cultural and possibly even spiritual experience kids have as they make connections with their local habitats, come to care about the health and well-being of a particular place and gain the ecological literacy that helps them articulate this.

A range of environmental groups are doing similar engaged-knowing projects. In the US, Bee Haven International has enlisted citizen scientists to monitor local bio-spheric conditions to track and help restore bee pollinator health.[5] Water-research.net supplies materials for water testing and information for monitoring local water conditions and watershed management.[6] (As an aside, a group of citizen scientists collecting data on noise levels near a scrapyard in the London district of Deptford, England, succeeded in demonstrating that the yard violated noise limits, and the UK Environment Agency revoked the scrapyard's license.)[7] Knowledge is power, which is also why it's also so political.

In North America, citizen science is especially urgent these days when a dramatic shutdown of government-funded common good and public interest research, and the laying off of the credentialed scientists who have done this work, is leaving huge gaps in knowledge and knowing. A survey of citizen science, which has been on the rise in this climate of chill and cutbacks, uncovered a number of long-standing programs, some with hundreds of citizen volunteer-participants, a high rate of sustained commitment and the successful public dissemination of results. A standardized and sometimes downloadable training program for citizen participants was also identified as critical, and among the top recommendations, along with collaboration with experts throughout.[8]

The revival of traditional farming knowledge practices is part of an alternative farming model associated with agroecology and a general shift to diversified farming practices. Both are described in academic literature as "knowledge rich" and "created in common and used in common" between farmers. In the US, several regional and even national networks, including the National Young Farmers' Coalition, support peer-to-peer learning. In California too, a number of small agroecological partnerships have developed bringing together producers, University of California-based researchers and county extension staff. They're trying to "rebuild traditional models of extension around greater participation by producers in designing, testing and evaluating agroecological practices." However, the long-standing pattern of experts and dependency still holds. Despite decades of reports urging agricultural extension programs in the US to treat farmers as participants and to support sustainable agriculture, "farmers are rarely treated as collaborative partners who can produce their own credible, scientifically meaningful knowledge." A 2010 National Academy of Science report on this noted "durable resistance" to wider notions of knowing.[9]

It's no surprise that the shift from a production model of knowing to a participant and commoning model is an ongoing challenge, because it's so critical to make alternative models of doing things (including running economies and societies) real. It's important, therefore, that activist groups and NGOs who are committed to change make this part of their own change agenda: helping their members move beyond moments of protest toward more implicated participation, becoming participant knowers and knowledgeable participants of change, as Food Secure Canada did in the extensive, participatory and inclusive (with First Nations communities playing a prominent role) discussion process used in developing its People's Food Policy, and with important support from the Centre for Studies in Food Security at Ryerson University in Toronto.[10] There are many resources groups would tap into in purusing this sort of participatory initiative, some associated with promoting citizen-led development and change internationally. In Canada, there's the Coady International Institute I mentioned earlier and the International Development Research Centre. The Institute for Development Studies at the University of Sussex in the UK is another rich source. Then there are networks like the Global Alliance on Community-Engaged Research (GACER) and the Development Research Centre on Citizenship, Participation and Accountability (DRC).[11] Founded in 2001, the DRC is a network of academics, activists and knowledge practitioners from universities and think tanks in seven core countries, with dozens of others involved as well. In its first ten years, it gathered information on a range of alternative, democratic knowledge creation and co-creation methods, including popular theater and participatory action research. Reviewing these, it identified some core principles that set these practices apart from the mainstream of knowledge creation. One is the value of co-constructing knowledge collaboratively, not through hierarchies of authority between expert researchers and the objects of their research in the field. Another core principle is the importance of iterative ways of knowing (along the lines of the weak theorizing that J.K. Gibson-Graham endorse). Co-constructing knowledge opens an ongoing dialogue between generalized ideas and the particulars of context and habitat in the field, with no one possibly preconceived idea, or hypothesis, of what's real ruling the roost.[12] It can result, too, in more dynamic knowledge, more responsive to, and responsible toward, the particular contexts and habitats from which it derives.

In the process of embracing these more democratic methodologies, network members also found themselves adopting more democratic ways of governing themselves as a network — making it more decentralized and participatory. This required more time and attention to details of discussion, but also yielded closer relationships and trust. While practicing listening and other skills of oral literacy (something I'm implying here; it wasn't explicitly stated in the report), DRC members found themselves changing, becoming less self-centered and more attuned to others. At a retreat reflecting on all this, one researcher commented: "I don't know if I've become more political, but certainly I've become more sensitive. This whole culture of DRC — you have to be accountable ..." Others spoke of the need to be humble, "and in that humility comes the research encounter which allows one to learn and act with others." One researcher, from Mexico, saw a link between this humility and the ability to act on the core principles of collaboration and truly embrace the ongoing iteration between the conceptual and the contextual. "The iterative process is a way of humbling the conceptual frameworks and opening them up for different ways of working," and with this comes a "humbling of the academic community and ... academic practices." Participant researchers, with healthy, humble egos, can embrace shifting their sense of self from a "public intellectual" to a "participatory intellectual."[13] In other words, recovering experts like me can move from having to be masters in a debating forum of experts to being participants in a commons of open-minded listening and collaborative, weak theorizing, accountable to the context at hand.

Some of these centers have week-long and longer residential learning programs; this is important for people to gain self-confidence as knowledgeable participants, and also to develop skills in leadership from within to help people mobilize the shared knowledge toward action and actionable policy. The Highlander Folk School in the US has long specialized in this kind of citizen leadership for change. During the civil rights movement of the 1960s and '70s, people like Rosa Parks spent time there learning about leadership from within a situation that needs to change, and how to claim that power and act on it (including on a city bus).[14] In Canada, the Canadian Labour Congress runs a labor college at Port Elgin, Ontario and while they've traditionally focused mainly on leadership training within the workplace, this will likely broaden as the merger between the Canadian Auto Workers and the Communications, Energy and Paperworkers Union of Canada into Unifor introduces a new focus on community to the union mandate. Meanwhile, the Coady Institute has downloadable research and knowledge-building tools to help community and other groups organize themselves into participatory action. One of these is called "Asset-Based Community Development," (ABCD) which can help people map the various assets participants bring to a potential action project, including formal and informal associations, so that they can use local resources and retain control over what they undertake. This package has been used to good effect in community economic development projects in Africa, in partnerships between Coady, Oxfam and the Comart Foundation, which specializes in supporting community-led development.[15] But I think its lessons are transferrable to activist groups associated with social and environmental justice.

There is another element — forming what is called a *knowledge commons* — that's as important as cultivating common, participatory knowledge and affirming people as knowledgeable participants capable of acting on their insider's sense of what's real and what has to change. In this second aspect, we share our storied knowledge, combining it with more objective reductive knowledge where relevant, and build a common pool of knowledge that will inform participatory policy discussions and action. Such knowledge commons can be a database for open access to knowledge that's already been produced and packaged (e.g. articles, reports) by NGOs and independent, alternative media, like *Watershed Sentinel* and *The Aboriginal People's Television Network* (APTN), various media co-ops, such as the *Halifax Media Co-op*, online publications like Rabble.ca and community computer networks that have emerged since the 1980s like Digital City Amsterdam, the Seattle Community Network and several similar ones in Canada, including the *Kuh-ke-nah Network* (K-net) in Northwest Ontario that links over 100 "points of presence" in Aboriginal communities and organizations across Ontario, Manitoba and Quebec.[16] Knowledge commons can also be a discussion platform for building weak theories of change, drawing in various activist groups and NGOs as participants in developing consensus around policies and plans for action. The International Association for the Study of the Commons operates as a knowledge commons, offering a huge digital library, with advanced search tools through its website.[17] This database is open to all, both to contribute pieces of knowledge they think fit the commons frame of reference, and to receive.

Wikipedia in particular and the Google-enhanced web generally are other examples of knowledge commons, as is the Public Library of Science and the Creative Commons where people (including me) deposit material they've written freeing people from copyright restrictions but also holding them accountable to honor the work's integrity.[18] Then, there are the free and readily accessible materials available through a range of organizations with an online presence, from environmental groups like Greenpeace, the Sierra Club, the David Suzuki Foundation to the Worldwatch Institute, the Earth Policy Institute, the Canadian Centre for Policy Alternatives and the Pembina Institute in Alberta. Then there are organizations focused on one specific thing like water, forestry, mining and food. In the area of food alone, groups that have collected knowledge range from Food Secure Canada and the Northern Health Food Initiative (among aboriginal communities) to Food First: Institute for Food and Development Policy, the Pesticide Action Network International, Agroecology.org. And I haven't even touched on ones operating in French, Spanish and other languages! I don't know how much this knowledge is also linked to policy discussion and action, along the lines of this being envisaged at least in The Pod Knowledge Exchange associated with Community Food Centres Canada, an NGO that Nick Saul has launched that provides a forum for sharing experience and learnings from one community food center to another.[19]

This is an important next step of activist groups' action: not just gathering knowledge to make a case for government action, but to inform actions their members might undertake, possibly in solidarity with other groups more directly affected by, for instance, toxins in local drinking water or toxic seepage from bitumen tailing ponds. Local chapters of the Council of Canadians are an interesting example of this new phase of implicated action. In Winnipeg, for instance, the local chapter became knowledgeable about plans to turn control over the city's water and wastewater services to a public-private partnership with Veolia, a multinational water company, and led public actions to stop it.[20] In Germany, the fruit-tree identification website Mundraub I mentioned earlier is using the principle of crowd sourcing which is collaborative and self-organizing. Anyone who finds a local fruit tree can become involved, first just naming it and its location so it can be tagged on the site. Surprisingly, though, people are continuing to monitor the trees they've located, building up shared knowledge about them and shared responsibility too. More than once, a find spot has been taken off the web platform at the request of users concerned that it not be overused. According to Katharina Frosch, an innovation economist and co-founder of mundraub (which won sustainability awards in 2010 and 2011), the self-organized knowledge that is being developed through the fruit-tree website is allowing its participants to "overtake responsibility for the fruity abundance."[21]

It's important that we scale up this knowledge sharing into intentional knowledge commons in specific policy areas (such as food, water, air) with these commons intentionally building a model of knowledge that draws on all four streams of knowing and related literacy that I discussed in Chapters 14, 15 and 16: the oral and ecological as well as text and data. Paralleling this, it's equally important to link progressive policy initiatives to these supportive knowledge bases so that our common knowledge can inform and support these policy alternatives. Charles Schweik, a professor of public policy at the University of Massachusetts who was among the first recipients of the Elinor Ostrom Award on Collective Governance, is involved in a citizen science project called "early detection, rapid response" in which people help monitor invasive plants and insects using a smart phone app called "Outsmart" and an online database.[22] Through his own networks and also the website knowledgecommons.net, Professor Schweik hopes he and his colleagues can "port their collaborative principles into other domains (less populated by highly tech savvy people) like public policy."[23] Claiming our agency as participants in situations, communities and habitats who become responsibly knowledgeable about them is a huge first step towards reclaiming the commons. Next, we must claim our responsibility to act on what we know as knowledgeable participants to bring about corrective change for the common good.

23

Re-enfranchising People as Commoners, Participants in Responsible Self-Governance

Hᴏᴡ ᴄᴀɴ ᴡᴇ ᴇꜰꜰᴇᴄᴛ ᴍᴇᴀɴɪɴɢꜰᴜʟ ᴄʜᴀɴɢᴇ without address-ing the long, slow disenfranchisement of people as responsible participants in the governance and operation of their society? These days in North America, democratic participation means voting in mi-cro-managed elections, a scope so limited that most people no longer bother going out to vote. It's far from the local self-governing autonomy of our ancestors on the commons as I detailed this, and its loss, in Part I. Restoring governance for a common good that includes the well-being of the whole planet will require revitalizing democracy at every level. And this means reclaiming not just the power of agency in self-gover-nance but organizations, institutional practices, skills and discipline as well as the time required for this to happen. The move to embrace a new model of governance was perhaps the core agenda of the Occupy Movement and perhaps also one of the reasons for the huge public support it gained. Occupy touched a hunger for alternatives to an in-creasingly remote, business-oriented and bureaucratized government on the one hand and the increasing corporatization of society on the other.

The resurgent popularity of the Commons speaks to the same hun-ger. Most commons operating at least in Europe and Asia in the 1960s and 1970s were remnants of premodern times, organized around the sharing of grazing lands, water for irrigation, wildlife, fisheries and for-ests, and only somewhat in the social organization of communities and villages (as in India, for example). Today, the term Commons is being applied to a huge range of activity and thought, from community gar-dens, homeowners' and tenants' associations, to open-access software and databases on the Internet, nonprofit organizations, public domain knowledge and ecotourism and, globally, commons of biodiversity, public health, water basin protection, Antarctica and the Atmosphere.[1] In *The Wealth of the Commons*, co-editors David Bollier and Silke Helfrich enthuse that "It is a discourse that transcends and remakes the categories of the prevailing political and economic order. It provides us with a new socially constructed order of experience ... and a persuasive grand narrative."[2] Still, enacting this narrative, even getting the story line up and the grammar worked out, is easier said than done. One of the reasons Elinor Ostrom was awarded the Nobel Prize in Economics for her work on the Commons is that she addressed the gap in theorizing to support any organizational and governance option other than either the market or the state, both featuring "outside control," as she put it. The common sense of our time still tends not to credit self-organized con-trol by insiders, particularly in economic areas where self-interest often rules. "That's too romantic to succeed! It's unrealistic!" The spin-doc-toring legacy of the so-called tragedy of the commons continues.

Yet proof is accumulating. There is now a growing body of theory identifying and corroborating the core principles that make the com-mons organizational model a sustainable alternative to the status quo in managing natural resources like water, woods and pastureland — if not yet oil and gas as well. These organizational principles include:

1. Clearly defining boundaries, both on who are the insiders, the participants in a particular commons, and what resource or area is included.

2. Mutually agreeing on rules, including stints or limits, on using irrigation water, and harvesting fish or trees. The stints or quotas are essential to address what's called the free rider problem and,

with it, the danger of pushing the commons beyond its carrying capacity. It's also important that these rules are responsive to the realities of the larger environment in which the commons is situated, including larger-scale government environments.

3. Monitoring both the condition of the commons and participants' use of it, through elected/appointed monitors or collaborative, participative methods, to ensure that the rules are being followed and that the commons remains healthy and its population of fish or trees remains sustainable. It's important that this knowledge be available to all, including evidence of someone exceeding their stint or quota.

4. Having real and enforceable, though usually graduated, sanctions for rule breakers is critical too. (In Switzerland where the uplands pasture commons have persisted from premodern times to the present, village courts impose fines on those who exceed their allotted grazing rights, their stint or quota on how many cattle can be sent to the common pasture.)[3]

5. A broader dispute- and conflict-resolution mechanism is often also necessary because real life in living habitats is complex, and can give rise to conflicting interpretation of rules under different circumstances. (In the Valencia region of Spain, regular tribunals hear and resolve disputes that arise over water use before they escalate, threatening the integrity of the commons and participants' trust in it.)[4]

6. It's critical too that the autonomy and local governing authority of the commons be recognized by external authorities.

7. It's often useful to nest this local self-governance within a polycentric scheme with different levels of authority taking on different aspects of responsibility.[5]

There's nothing romantic about this model of governance. In one of the last speeches Elinor Ostrom gave before her death in 2012, she stressed the mutual reinforcement of commons practices: that people tend to trust a situation where they know rules are being honored because they're being monitored (and everyone quickly knows who's breaking them). And they can trust the rules because the people making them and modifying them are also the ones most knowledgeable about the local situation.[6]

Trust and a shared sense of community follow, she and others have learned, with these becoming the glue that sustains these enterprises over time.[7] These in turn are the cumulative effect of implicated participation: the gestalt of all that working together, sharing knowledge and responsibility and seeing the consequences of this on both the positive side and, no doubt, the negative as well. People come to be together-as-one with each other and the habitat on which they depend, as they did in premodern commons.

There are an expanding array of commoning enterprises around the world, sometimes called cooperative, sometimes co-management and sometimes more generally social enterprise. These models all involve participants in a situation or habitat working out how to organize and govern themselves through mutual obligation and mutual self-interest for the common good. In other words, participants are learning how to be responsible commoners.

Again and again, promising initiatives have emerged where there is a clear gap in public services or where local needs are demonstrably not being met. The self-governing powers the James Bay Cree in Canada have achieved through the James Bay and Northern Quebec Agreement is an example. The James Bay Cree (the Cree Nation of *Eeyou Istchee*) didn't achieve effective self-determination in the initial agreement with governments worked out in 1975, under the smart, young leadership of Billy Diamond, though the groundwork was laid in this historic treaty-like document which recognized the Cree nation's right to sustain their traditional way of life in return for allowing hydro-dam development on their traditional territory. It required many years of intense lobbying and court action to negotiate a transfer of authority and funding from both the federal and provincial governments to enlarge the scope of local self-governance to include education and social services plus economic and community development. Under the equally smart leadership of another grand chief, Matthew Coon Come, they also blocked a planned second phase of the hydro development project in their territory because it threatened the Cree way of life and the carrying capacity of both the local habitat and local communities.[8]

In the Northwest Territories, an area sacred to the local Délįnę (*Sahyoue* and *Edacho*, two peninsulas reaching into *Sahtu*, or Great Bear Lake) has been designated a National Historic Site to be used, shared and cared for by native and non-native inhabitants, with this co-managed by Parks Canada and Délįnę authorities. Moreover, Délįnę elders (including Morris Neyelle) led the collaborative discussions establishing the vision of this co-management, which includes the idea that caring for the land would imbue all actions, including harvesting of food, taken on it, as part of "our trail to travel on." Getting young people back onto the land, teaching them traditional survival and tracking skills is part of the vision, "to help the community be a community again."[9]

In the Central Pacific, the Micronesian island republic of Kiribati has, since gaining its independence from Britain in 1979, tooled its self-governance toward regenerating the local commons of the fishery. A trust fund created in the 1950s from royalties derived from foreign exploitation of the island's phosphate deposits has furnished the means for this. Ignoring the traditional "development" path of export-led growth (which would have focused on an infrastructure for export-market scale fishing), the government chose to instead use the trust fund to subsidize subsistence fishing and agriculture, and "replenishing its commons."[10]

In Nepal, forests had traditionally been a commons; they were only nationalized in 1957. Now, they are shifting back to local community control, partly because the government found it couldn't manage vast areas of woodland from afar. There are 16,000 community forest user groups managing 1.2 million hectares of land and benefitting some 1.7 million households, 32% of the population.[11] The right to local self-governance through these community user groups is formally recognized by the state, and includes the right to sanction members for breaking rules. Local self-governance also includes the responsibility for monitoring both members' use of the forest and its overall condition, and this is part of the participatory self-management. Shrikrishna Upadhyay, Right Livelihood Award winning author who's documented this, added: "Participatory Action Research (PAR) involving primary stakeholders is an essential part of this management model because community groups can build their capacities for self-governance only if they can build trust and reciprocity and enhance their ability to resolve inevitable problems and conflicts." Upadhyay went on to point out that not only are people able to make a living from the forest, sometimes launching community enterprises such as facilities to process medicinal herbs they've harvested. The community-managed forests are delivering on important conservation-like goals, such as carbon sequestering and higher-quality drinking water for downstream communities.[12]

The commons of the Earth will not, however, be reclaimed like a patchwork quilt, one self-governing local commons around water, woodlands or community enterprise at a time. At least I doubt it. A gestalt has to happen, tipping the paradigm away from running the world on economistic, rational self-interest principles and toward running it on common-good principles. Still, the stage for this to happen is set as more and more people participate in commons-framed projects and institutions, developing the self-organizing, self-governing skills and the general aptitude for mutuality within social and ecological habitats that is the hallmark of the commons. It's from this grounded and implicated participation that the ethos of the commons can come alive and grow strong enough to motivate commitment to common-good action and the confidence that this is doable. In Chapter 25, I will speculate on what some of those actions might be, from the microscale of local and personal habitats to the larger ones at issue in excessive carbon emissions and toxic overdevelopment. Here I want to focus more on the institution building and dialogue building that's required. Because what I said earlier, quoting Marilynne Robinson — about people not knowing their own minds but depending on others, experts, to tell them what's real and realistic — can be taken further. People often don't know their own habitat, their own world. Nor do they know their own power as implicated participants within it. But that can change if they team up with, talk with and take the time to work with others who also refuse to be passive but, instead, choose to be implicated.

The challenge for activist groups in the highly developed world where most people are several generations removed from an ancestral, customary claim to the land or water is to enact a claim to common in more indirect ways. In the previous chapter, I encouraged groups and NGOs to involve their membership in participatory knowing and learning so that they not only generate useful and even actionable knowledge but become knowledgeable participants, confident in what they know and say. Now the challenge is to take participation further, into action projects and policy discussions. One helpful step toward this might involve addressing the roots of the global and local activist divide, or "two solitudes" in Naomi Klein's words. From my own experience in both solitudes, I suspect that the divide between them has a lot to do with lines of communication. Because global groups came of age focused on changing macro policies, their communication was vertical and often directed to remote centers of power. Local groups' lines were almost the opposite: more horizontal and often confined to the local community, even one issue. There's been a shift away from this in recent decades, toward more of a mix of the two. Still, more of this mixing is needed, and perhaps can be pursued intentionally. One possibility is that in cities and towns where some groups have already come together in shared, common space, this collective, or one group within it, can take the initiative to organize a local forum for talking about collaboration in some local action and more global discussions about the policies that are involved. Over time, this commoning space could become the equivalent of the commons-promoting office in the Berlin municipal government. Meanwhile, starting small, the idea would be that local members of a range of groups, local and global, could get involved in common cause initiatives that are grounded locally. That way, too, when larger-scale policy discussions occur, it's easier for everyone to link the global with the local and vise versa. Participants would bring their nuanced understanding of the local, along with their experience reconciling contradictions in real-life situations and the patience that working in the real world requires, to larger discussions. They could also bring a level of self-confidence as change agents speaking for the commons — and perhaps be less easily sidelined or undermined by spin doctors of the status quo. In Ottawa, what was originally called Under One Roof and now 25OneCommunity is an example of such a common-ground space that could serve as a nucleus for commoning initiatives. It is shared office space in the downtown core of Ottawa, cohabited by the Canadian Centre for Policy Alternatives (CCPA), the Canadian Health Coalition (CHC), Friends of the Earth (FOE), a number of union locals, a lawyer specializing in charities, plus an independent bookstore (Octopus), an alternative indie media (Rabble. ca) and, as of 2014, the Council of Canadians. The initiative came from Diane Touchette, Director of Operations with the CCPA, which regularly sponsors conferences, symposia and the like from its offices across the country. Her dream was to take this further, into a "common cause initiative," a bit like the Centre for Social Innovation in Toronto.[13] It would be good if a faith group were present, and perhaps a local office of Idle No More and the new union organization, Unifor (whose mandate is the formation of community chapters with a focus on both people's workplace and the community as a whole). Meanwhile, I'm sure more such common-ground local space sharing will emerge, especially if the notion of commoning locally and networking commons-reclaiming policies globally takes off. The important thing is to follow the commoning process, which involves doing everything in shares, as a team, with leadership from within. This way, too, no one person is responsible, and no one has to focus obsessively on the outcome. Instead, everyone is free to stay grounded in the here and now, in relating to each other and the realities of the habitat or situation at hand. Let's say the CCPA or the CHC or FOE took the initiative and issued a blanket invitation to any and all organizations in a range of social and environmental justice concerns to invite their local members to attend a monthly brown-bag lunch. Or the Octopus Book Store could turn a book launch in the shared space into a launching pad of discussion. What can we do together? Using asset mapping, what strengths and skills and resources can we pool together? A viable project might emerge around water, with the local Riverkeeper identifying a project that involves more people in local water testing or shoreline cleanup. Or community health centers might collaborate with the West End Well (food) Co-op to expand access to locally sourced fresh vegetables in a low-income neighborhood perhaps also housing a lot of recent refugee immigrants, out of which a cross-cultural gardening common might emerge. Members from relevant groups and NGOs with relevant knowledge and skills would team up, identifying tasks to be done, from research to stick handling through bureaucratic red tape to tapping local sources of material and funding and drawing in people to advise on any research and knowledge gathering involved. Responsibility to organize and lead a next meeting would be shared among the groups, constantly reinforcing the commoning principle of mutual obligation, that the buck of responsibility stops with all of them. Success, in other words, rests with the participants and their implicated participation at every level from the concrete actions they're undertaking to their attentive observation and learning as they go and the sharing of these insights in the day to day shared governance of the project. NGOs that operate with a model of a core of paid staff and a host of volunteers, or like a community center with services delivered to the public, might start to reinvent themselves along a more commons model, with volunteers becoming participants increasingly sharing responsibility with paid staff.

This emerging identity as an implicated participant in a common-good cause needs then to be affirmed in the realm of language and culture, especially in discussions where the participants in local commoning projects can in turn participate in policy discussions. Here, an organization like the Council of Canadians could take the lead, perhaps using the teach-in tool that they used in discussions opposing the expansion of corporate governance through so-called free trade deals. The council, which allied itself in solidarity with the Idle No More

Movement when it emerged in December 2012, could also network with the Aboriginal community and, in collaboration with the CCPA perhaps, organize a participant conference on self-determination and self-governance. Imagine such a conference, cosponsored by the Grand Council of the Cree or the Assembly of First Nations, where Grand Chief Matthew Coon Come would sit at the same round table with a tenants' council representative from Toronto, someone from Nuestras Raices in Massachesetts, someone from the KOFAR collective in Haiti (see Chapter 21) and someone associated with the self-managed forestry in Nepal, with each person telling their particular story of self-determining, self-governing success. In order to advance reclaiming the commons and the ethos of the common good as its governing principle, what's essential is that any self-governing policy discussion be grounded in implicated participation. It must be centered in the here and now of real-life situations requiring change and healing, with the direct agency of those involved present and the lines of accountability following similar centered lines, back to the here and now.

24

The Commons as Culture, Community and Creation

RECLAIMING THE COMMONS IS NOT JUST A CAUSE OR SOCIAL MOVE-MENT, though it certainly is that. Nor is it a box in some attic one opens and, voilà, the commons is instantly revived, ready for all to enjoy. As Nicholas Blomley, a geographer who's written about the premodern commons and suggested instances where commoning might be at work today, has pointed out: "The commons isn't so much found as produced." He went on to note that "If it is true to say that place helps make the commons, it is equally the case that the commons is a form of place making."[1] It's making a place, first as imagined, drawing perhaps on ancestral memories, then through shared activities, discussion and commitment. It's also community building in the fullest sense of the word. As we enter more fully as participants in this, we enlarge our sense of self as shared and vested in relationships of mutual support. We can also expand our sense of home, and feeling at home, to include not just the local neighborhood and habitat where we live but the larger home of the Earth.

Having parties, street dances, poetry readings, song and poetry-writing workshops and festivals full of local food, food growers and makers, games for the kids and adults too, readings, talks, singing and dancing is fun. Not only is having fun a virtue, according to theologian Matthew Fox, founder of Creation Spirituality and coauthor of *Occupy*

Spirituality. It's also a way to complete the process of biomapping described earlier. Here, people get to bring themselves as whole human beings into the scene, along with a range of talents other than what's important for organizing a protest, writing a brief or discussing points of policy. Ritual is important too — shared motions, songs, meaningful words. According to African ritual teacher, Melidoma Some, "there is no community without ritual."[2] But to be authentic, ritual has to emerge from within the community, perhaps in the context of some shared action around water, or trees or growing food; a ritual expressing gratitude perhaps, or a yearning for reconciliation. Otherwise, it can be the same old thing, of people being told what to do, or even how to feel. We also need our own songs! The Labor movement, especially during the hungry 1930s, had its songs that were sung around campfires and marches to nations' capitols. The Civil Rights Movement had its songs that bound people together on the street and sometimes too in jail. The most famous is probably "We Shall Overcome," which started as a draft that two unknown union members from South Carolina brought to the Highlander Folk School in the 1940s, and which the school administrator's wife, Zilphia Horton, turned over to Pete Seeger during one of his regular visits to the school, hoping he could shape the words and tune into something that might catch on.[3]

As the sense of community and sustained participation in events both serious and frivolous grows, some group within the common-space circle that's been part of this — a community health center, for instance, or faith group — might take the lead in fostering meditation sessions or discussion groups around personal growth and healing. As I've said repeatedly throughout this book, to reconnect with the Earth we must first and also reconnect with ourselves. Or as Matthew Fox put it in telling his own story in *Occupy Spirituality*: "If you don't work on yourself, then much of your politics is merely projection. We have to walk our talk, and do the inner work that allows the outer work to be authentic and also effective."[4]

Perhaps there's a way to learn from the tradition of consulting with elders and grandmothers/grandfathers in First Nations communities where it's an integral part of the Idle No More Movement. Or perhaps the tradition of the anam cara or soul friend that was so vital for cultivating character and a commitment to the common good in Celtic Christianity can be revived. Or perhaps chaplains and an increasing array of others who are bringing the practice and discussion of faith and spirituality outside formal religious institutions, in retreat centers or through the Base Communities movement, can play a role. Tom Sherwood, an Ottawa-based minister, ended a long career as a university chaplain with a three-year study that drew more than 300 Canadian university students from a variety of faith backgrounds into a dialogue about their spirituality. What he found, in a nutshell, is that the so-called Net Generation or the Millennial and also the Echo Generation (born between 1980 and 1995) is not religious (something they associate with organized churches), but is very spiritual. For these people, faith is very personal. It's also grounded in personal growth and in the real world, including nature. For Sherwood, this generation is expressing a new "religious literacy" ... one that I'm tempted to call eco-spiritual if not 'eco-theological. They're also, he wrote, articulating "new positions on the spiritual landscape."[5] Or perhaps they are refusing the modern era's long exile from nature's landscape into hierarchial church organizations, and returning to the original landscape, Creation itself, and embracing what Black American mystic Howard Thurman referred to as the God of Life, versus the God of Religion.[6]

If reclaiming the commons is also about embracing our place within it, developing what could be called a commons consciousness might include embracing being an implicated participant in Creation itself. Spirituality, having played a major role in forging the nature-culture divide in ways I alluded to in Chapter 17, has a role to play in healing it too. In fact, reconciliation is a major theme in a wealth of new thinking and action at work under the names of Creation Spirituality, eco-theology, ecofeminism and a lot of New Age spirituality generally. Some ideas draw from the breakthrough vision of quantum physics: the radical interconnectedness of space and time and equally profound realization that matter cannot be wholly separated from the energy that moves and shapes it. As Fritjof Capra put it, popularizing this new (and very old) understanding of reality's foundations, "As we penetrate into matter, nature does not show us any isolated 'basic building blocks,' but rather appears as a complicated web of relations between the various parts of the whole."[7] Ecofeminists such as Carolyn Merchant and Susan Griffin have drawn lines of identification between the objectification and subjugation of woman and of nature, and articulate a double refusal of this, asserting the voice and agency of both.

A lot of new effort and thinking is also coming out of traditional faith traditions, including Hindu and Muslim, Jewish and Christian, sometimes remaining rooted there, sometimes embracing a new concept called eco-theology. In a series of books including *Original Blessing* and *A Spirituality Named Compassion* which lay out the basis for Creation Spirituality, Matthew Fox drew on both the recent lessons of postmodern physics and ancient traditions of the Old Testament to make a case for connection and compassion as the essence of spiritual practice. Citing numerous Biblical passages, from Acts for example, he argued that Judaism and Christianity were meant to be *ways of life* (emphasis mine), not religions separate from daily life. One of these ways was maintaining a weekly day of rest, and including domestic animals in this time of repose. Another practice was ensuring that domestic animals were fed ahead of humans. Fox quoted the 14th-century mystic Meister Eckhart who championed the Golden Rule of "love thy neighbor as thyself" as compassion born of simple identification. "What happens to another, whether it be joy or sorrow, happens to you." Fox linked this rule to the new physics: "Instead of a 'cloudy humanitarianism' that distance and objectivity dictate, the new physics suggests a physically rooted self-interest as the key to morality, for what happens to another happens to us all."[8]

In the faith tradition I'm part of, healing and reconciliation in the here and now are important themes, and evident as a strong faith presence in social justice and environmental justice work. I think of this shift as moving away from atonement to a remote judgmental god toward becoming attuned to the Spirit of Life present and alive in all

Creation. This shift is not necessarily confined to church communities either; nor does it require a belief in something called God. It does require a place for faith or spirituality in your life, however. The only other thing it requires, at least according to the philosopher Ronald Dworkin in his posthumously published 2013 book *Religion Without God*, is the belief or faith that "nature — the universe as a whole and in all its parts — is not just a matter of fact but is itself sublime: something of intrinsic value and wonder."[9] Connecting with that, tuning into that, is what matters.

There are self-help books galore and personal growth literature as well as many other avenues through which people are pursuing spiritual connection in their lives. Many young people are doing it by direct implication in the world, as activists. For example, Adam Bucko, who came of age through Poland's Solidarity Movement, spent time in an ashram and studied theology, works with homeless street kids in New York City through a facility he cofounded, called the Reciprocity Foundation. In *Occupy Spirituality*, which he coauthored with Matthew Fox, he referred to his work as spiritual democracy and mentoring. "I moved from a spirituality of detachment to a spirituality of integration," he wrote, adding that "My God lives on the street."[10] A 2013 article called "The United Church Diaspora" published in the *United Church Observer* showcased a number of young people who are active in community organizing, anti-poverty work and the environment. Few attend church today, but they all grew up in one, and partly credit this for their activist engagement. Christine Boyle, a community organizer in Vancouver who wrote the piece, found that what these young people most cherished from growing up going to church wasn't the Bible texts or other church liturgy. It was the shared activities and loving community of the congregation.[11] Their church modeled how to live in empathetic and compassionate community with others, how to live as an implicated participant in the habitats of our world.

You can't feel such connection by remote observation, only by participation. Only by opening your eyes to really see, by opening your ears to truly listen and take in whatever it might be — the suffering of another, anger at injustice, sounds of a watershed running amok — can you begin to implicate yourself in the larger whole of our social and natural environment. You need personal courage and conviction to take this on, to open your heart and spirit to the possibilities, the dangers and the responsibilities of connection.

Retreat centers and study centers also have a role to play; many are run by progressive theologians and ecophilosophers. Developing spiritual connection involves being present and becoming attuned to yourself, others and the larger living world as a way of life. It also takes time to get to this point. Perhaps you have to heal the disconnect you've been living. Perhaps you need to unplug yourself from too much immersion in online connectivity, to declutter your life so you can become implicated in the here and now off screen. There are two things that matter here, and I notice that they're priorities in both native and non-native faith traditions. The first is empathy or compassion — the ability to feel for the other, and the second, related to this, is humility. Nuu-chah-nulth philosopher Richard Atleo identified this as critical to the successful function of at least one of the four constitutional principles he named in *The Principles of Tsawalk: An Indigenous Approach to Global Crisis*: mutual recognition if not also respect.[12]

In Chisasibi on James Bay, Quebec, Abraham Bearskin, an elder working for the Cree Board of Health and Social Services who I met by the Sacred Fire outside the Truth and Reconciliation Hearings in Montreal, is applying spiritual principles to everyday life in the commons of his community. He has been tasked with integrating traditional *Nishiyuu* teachings into the health and social service programs the board provides. *Nishiyuu* means "spirit of the people," including all peoples, all races. It's understood as a bloodline of traditions and teachings which each generation is responsible for passing on in appropriate form to the next. Bearskin learned these traditions from what he calls "the old ones," and it's now his turn. He organizes and leads traditional healing and spiritual growth rituals such as the sweat lodge, the shaking tent and the sun dance. Now, incorporating the teachings into, for example, the practice of midwifery, he's focusing on the spiritual counseling component, which includes helping the future father understand that he is pregnant too. "You have to feel for the life inside," he explained, adding that there are protocols for both the man and the woman to follow so you "don't disturb the growth of life."

He comfortably and matter-of-factly told me: "I am one with the land," and "the land is a healer; that's our hospital." Abraham Bearskin takes time to go out on the land on a regular basis, opening himself to what the animals and plants, rocks and creeks have to teach him. "You never graduate from there. You never get a paper," he said, laughing. "But you get something, unexplainable." Bearskin called it "spirit wisdom" and then explained that as he's come to understand it, "when you're talking about spirit, you're dealing with feelings, with energy. You have to know that to make it work."[13]

Becoming attuned to others in the shared habitats of life on Earth: It's that simple and that mysterious.

Common-Good Governance
Locally and Globally

T HERE IS A GAP IN THEORIZING ABOUT THE GOVERNANCE OF
SOCIETY similar to the one over options for running an economy
(state versus market) that Elinor Ostrom and others have worked so
hard to fill. In fact, there's almost a gap in even imagining other alternatives. Moral philosopher George Lakoff parsed the choices, in
American politics at least, as between a stern father exhorting rugged
self-sufficiency (associated with conservatives) or a nurturing mother
(associated with liberals). When it comes to Creation, nature and the
environment, the Strict Father notion is premised on a "natural order
of domination," he wrote. "God has dominion over human beings;
human beings over nature; parents over children; and so on."[1] Lakoff
quoted Newt Gingrich to drive home the consequences of this, saying
that for Gingrich, environmentalism starts with "man dominates the
planet" and only has a responsibility to "minimize damage to the natural world."[2] The Nurturing Mother tries to offset this: depicting nature
as nurturing mother and divine being to be revered and respected,
and also as home, as living organism and as victim needing to be protected.[3] The liberal position is the most hopeful, Lakoff argued, being
the source of institutions like the Environmental Protection Agency
and the Endangered Species Act. Both, however, view nature from the

outside, unlike the commons, which at least partly views it from within, from the perspective of implicated participants.

And so for me, the commons model offers a hopeful third choice: re-enfranchising people as responsible co-participants in the governance of the larger habitats that sustain them, including in their individual lives. In this approach, we are not left to help ourselves on our own, nor are we waiting to be rescued and looked after — but come together in various commoning and common cause arenas to share looking after the larger whole of community and habitat. Reclaiming the commons, claiming a shared responsibility to restore right human relations with the larger commons of Earth, requires restoring responsible common-good self-governance from the local habitat of community and community institutions on up.

A lot of what I've been suggesting so far is preparation and capacity building for this. It's about placemaking as I said, quoting Nicholas Blomley, earlier: claiming our place as part of the picture from the local to the global. The commoning model offers a way to organize ourselves, developing and sharing knowledge and articulating relevant policies, where the mutual obligation and mutual self-interest of commons self-governance come together around right relations with others and the habitat. Commoning involves a lot of what has long been associated with community development, particularly in its current form. It involves people taking up the power of agency that is latent in every situation requiring change and becoming implicated participants in changing the status quo.

This is the activism of the Zapatistas, inspired in part by the liberation theology of some of the Catholic agencies who worked with their early leaders. According to the WSM (Workers' Solidarity Movement) website's entry on this grassroots movement in which local indigenous people are reclaiming local land, "the purpose of the organization is not to seize power on behalf of the people — rather it is to create a space in which people can define their own power."[4] It's not power over but power to, which Judy Rebick talks about in her book *Transforming Power*. It's the power to act on shared conviction and alternative vision, informed by knowledge and policy choices appropriate to these. As John Gaventa, Director of the Coady Institute, put it in *Global Citizen Action*, "An understanding of citizenship as participation puts less emphasis on rights as entitlements to be bestowed by a nation state ... and more on ... responsible action.... through the process of citizen action, or human agency, itself."[5]

The challenge facing us as implicated citizens is huge: Confronting not only the failures to mitigate let alone reverse the carbon and temperature arithmetic of climate change, but the relentlessness of the dynamo driving it. This dynamo includes not just the scale and power of global corporations with their often overlapping boards of directors. There's also the growing number of people who've invested in them and who depend on wealth through returns on that investment for their income. As Benjamin M. Friedman wrote "the balance between income from work and income from wealth ... is shifting. The share coming from wealth now stands at a record high."[6] That's a powerful concentration of vested interest in keeping the pipelines of investment and returns on investment flowing full and fast, with these in turn driving supply pipelines, production and distribution pipelines, merchandising and promotion pipelines and, of course, oil and gas pipelines, running through our backyards.

It's over the basic necessities of life that the contradictions are coming into sharp relief, the well-being of people and the well-being of the Earth equally put at risk. Safe, healthy food within reach of everyone and safe, healthy water within reach of everyone are under threat. Safe, clean air that people need to breathe every minute of their lives can no longer be taken for granted. Asthma has become a major disease throughout the developed world. In China, 1.2 million premature deaths reported in 2010 were attributed to air pollution.[7] A huge gap in common-good governance has allowed these things to happen.

These are also realities to which many people in North America can relate: how their and their families' personal habitats have been poisoned or jeopardized. These are realities around which people can potentially mobilize, discussing and agreeing on policy alternatives and

identifying what needs to be done. As Diana Bronson, executive director of Food Secure Canada, told me: "Everyone has a personal food
policy: fast, slow, cheap or organic, and everyone can engage around
that."[8] Food is a place to start implicating people in the choices being
made by corporations and government agencies, making the connections between the personal and the political.

The next step is to get people exploring what food is and means,
what clean water and air mean too, using participant knowledge practices of the sort I discussed in Chapter 22. Any number of the NGOs
involved in these basic issues could take some of the initiative here.
Pursuing the food theme in Canada, this might mean Food Secure
Canada teaming up with a local food bank, community health center or the Council of Canadians, with its largely self-governing local
chapters across the country in applying the principles of the People's
Food Policy. The Prince Albert, Saskatchewan chapter, for example,
has helped promote partnerships between local sources of food and
local institutions that can use it. It's also part of the Prince Albert Food
Coalition, which persuaded City Council to adopt a Food Charter
of Rights, which begins with a proclamation that "Every community
member has the basic right to a secure, affordable and nutritious food
supply, which is produced in an environmentally sustainable way."[9] In
one potential scenario, again in Canada, a local chapter of the Council
of Canadians might team up with the local office of the CCPA, plus
those active in local food security, to cosponsor community-based
teach-ins or discussion forums about food and health, drawing in
relevant knowledge, for example about the bottlenecks of vertical integration in food production that prevent local sourcing of produce
in most supermarkets, or the massive use of antibiotics in mass-pro-
duced livestock. The team might also connect with local scientists at
local universities and colleges (or perhaps retired ones) who could lead
the kind of objective data analysis that is required to complete a knowledge picture. What is the nutrient content of a factory-farm produced
carrot versus a local one grown using agroecological methods? What
is the carbon load in this steak produced in a chemical-intensive mass

feedlot, processed in a highly automated packing plant and transported thousands of kilometers to the local supermarket? What residues of antibiotics and other chemicals that might suppress immune systems are in this breast of chicken?

Part of commoning is reconnecting the dots of implication between an isolated consumer act and the habitat, social and natural, to which that economic act is linked, because disconnect is a core obstacle. The disconnect of the global economy from the larger contexts of life on Earth has become more than metaphoric in recent decades with the advent of nanosecond digital networks enabling its speed and reach. But the disconnect dates fundamentally back to the rise of the modern market-centered economy itself, when economic theory severed economics from the social relations of community and the ecological relations of habitat as its drivers and regulators. It seems that Aristotle foresaw the dangers of this disconnect even at the dawn of market economics in Ancient Athens. As Karl Polanyi interpreted this in *The Great Transformation*: "In denouncing the principle of production for profit as 'unnatural...,' boundless and limitless, Artistotle was, in effect, aiming at the crucial point, namely the divorcedness of a separate economic motive from the social relations in which these limitations inhered."[10] The ecological relations as well, I might add.

If something called a Reclaiming the Commons movement emerges, this is its agenda: to bring economic development back within the limitations inherent in nature; to re-position economics within the bounds of social and ecological relations. In other words, to dissolve the divorce and remarry economies to the carrying capacity of habitat, social and natural, so that both can be sustained in good heart. Developing participatory knowledge exercises in which people and local communities can connect the dots is part of such a movement. It helps close the distance between the global and the local, helps people come alive to the choices and trade-offs being made that they themselves are part of.

Take the fact that retail space per capita in the US doubled between 1990 and 2005, from 19 to 38 square feet.[11] Some local group associated with Sustainability or the Slow movement or transitioning to a

less carbon-intensive society could develop a downloadable DIY discussion kit that friends and co-workers could bring to a brown-bag
lunch, asking themselves how shopping-intensive their lives are, and
considering how personal overconsumption might be the consumer
counterpart to carbon intensity in the corporate economy. Connecting
the dots isn't always comfortable. As local citizens are drawn into the
creation of knowledge about the realities affecting their lives, as they
place themselves and their situation within the larger picture, they
might also begin to feel they have something to say about changing it,
and feel implicated enough to take action.

There are two trajectories of action I want to focus on as I end.
One is enlarging the scope and scale of commoning as placemaking
both for the sake of the land, the water and the air involved, and also
so that more people can have the direct experience of participating in
an actual commons and commons institution building. The other is
renewing a common-good political culture in which setting limits and
bounds on economic activity is seen as both normal and essential. In
other words, stinting as it was used to regulate the premodern economy of my ancestors, an economy centered in the local community and
the surrounding land. I talked about this, and its demise under the
forces of first the Agricultural and then the Industrial Revolution in
Part I, but also how this old order, and the attendant common sense
of what was normal, persisted. It also persisted in some 70 laws dating
back to the Tudor kings; these laws set limits on the emergent industrial economy to protect the traditional one organized around local
workshops and household manufacturing. According to an account of
these, excavated from the old statute books by British historian Adrian
Randall, one of these was an act "for the putting down of gig mills,"
a sheep-shearing frame through the use of which one man could do
the work of five. Another prohibited cloth manufacturers from owning
more than one loom. But in the early years of the 1800s, these old laws
were rescinded. And it was this deregulation, as much as the actual displacement caused by the industrial-scale machinery of the day, Randall
argued, that gave rise to the Luddite Movement. The word Luddite has

generally become a put-down, describing someone who blindly, stupidly resists progress — but that interpretation is largely the work of spin doctors like those who lent credence to "the tragedy of the commons." Randall's research (echoed by others, including E.P. Thompson in *The Making of the English Working Class*), suggested that the skilled craftspeople led by Ned Ludd weren't resisting change or progress as such. They "saw a role for capital in society, but within limits... [They] held an essentially moral view of economic relationships," causing them to resist and challenge what they saw as "the amoral economy of the innovators," Randall wrote.[12]

An organization like 350.org might well envision itself as a latter-day Luddite Movement, in the best sense of the word. They're not trying to stop progress, only redefine it as informed by the carrying capacity of this precious, fragile planet on which we all, and all progress, depend. The new normal 350.org is trying to inculcate is like that of our ancestors in the custom, community and land-based economies of their day: regulating the pace and scale of economic activity so as to sustain relations within the local habitat. It simply made sense to do this. It was normal.

Such thinking has been a long time fading and will take a while to revive, which is why linking the local and the global, the personal with the political, is so important. This is a challenge that organizations like 350.org with its global reach can take on as they continue to form common cause with more local groups on the ground. This and other progressive groups with global reach could take the lead facilitating action-related conversations about stinting that will restore the notion of limits to thinking about policy. At a personal level, stinting simply means living within one's means, and one's own ability to cope. At a local-to-regional, or institutional, corporate and community level, it means negotiating trade-offs and reconciling competing interests to stay within the carrying capacity of local watersheds and to conserve, and even honor, the local habitat. At a national and even global level, it means following the example of the Mackenzie Valley Pipeline Inquiry, where balancing the claims of developers against those of the habitat and its inhabitants resulted in slowing the pace of development in that watershed.

How can we do this? Slowly and incrementally, linking local discussions, local knowledge creation that combines personal stories and experience with science-grounded research, using all four elements of the knowledge model I described in Chapter 22. It's essential that we see ourselves as implicated participants, and our practices are essential to this: listening to each other, owning up to the contradictions within our lives and local situations, at work or elsewhere, we're part of; working together to make change, sharing responsibility; making a difference through local commoning or common cause efforts that inspire confidence to do more, in alliances with other groups, in solidarity with Aboriginal communities resisting toxic gold mine development, fracking on ancestral lands and free-for-all industrial-scale development of the Arctic.

The general assemblies of the Occupy Movement and the process associated with the World Social Forums offer models for advancing this, especially if they apply the lessons of the 2007 US Forum:

+ The first was to use the forum as a shared open space in which local grassroots activists could network and form alliances, sharing strategies on everything from food security to community/labor alliances to a new "taking back our cities" movement.

+ A related second aspect was ensuring that grassroots activists, speaking from their experience in the community-based organizations they represented, were at the center of the discussion, at plenaries as well as at workshops.[13]

Making a space for commons ways of thinking and acting in a world encased in self-interest, making money, dependence on experts and compliance with bureaucratic regulation is a formidable task. Having a commons, like the Gabriola Commons, in every community would therefore be useful. It's a living laboratory on how self-organizing, self-governing functions; it teaches the people who show up how to be implicated participants while also shedding light on the challenges that must be addressed in making real change. Such learning can then be applied to enlarging the scope of commoning, with citizen groups negotiating with local municipal governments to take over the management of public parks or other spaces and turn them into hubs of local food production as well as other community action.

In the area of extending the commons to bodies of water, what local residents of the Finger Lakes region of New York State recently did offers a useful success story. Here, a number of cooperative partnerships have formed to provide stewardship of watershed planning and management, building on strong local community associations around the various lakes involved. The Keuka Lake Association, formed in 1956 with nearly 2,000 members including local businesses as well as local citizens, emerged as the nucleus organization, "providing the vision, focus for cooperation, leadership and citizen support needed for watershed cooperation and protection," according to a report on this. Through fundraising efforts, they hired a "point person" with science and public-policy expertise to help move the necessary policy forward: a model wastewater law backed by the state and passed by all the municipalities affected by the watershed. But continuing local participation, and implication, was equally important because the model law involved an "aggressive inspection and maintenance program," and having local homeowners, with private septic systems, as well as local businesses, buy in as willingly compliant with this common-good initiative was essential.[14]

Perhaps this model can be used elsewhere — in Canada in the Comox Valley of BC where safe, healthy drinking water needs to be protected or in the Okanogan where over-irrigation has left the valley with no drinkable water in local wells or in Alberta where the whole Athabasca River watershed is at risk from the effects of bitumen extraction from the Tar Sands, and communities like Fort Chipewyan are falling sick from toxins in local waters. Collaboration might include local people associated with, for example, Pollution Probe, the David Suzuki Foundation, Greenpeace and the Council of Canadians, both nationally and as a local chapter. As a body of precedents builds, it will also build the public support and confidence required for larger initiatives: water basin commons, such as the Great Lakes and, perhaps one day, Antarctica and the Arctic. Maude Barlow, national chairperson of the Council of Canadians and former senior advisor on Water to the UN, is associated with the Great Lakes Basin Commons initiative, an effort to apply legal principles such as the public trust doctrine as well as the legacy of First Nations understanding of water to justify bringing the bioregion under protected common-good governance.[15]

There is a wealth of precedent out there to inspire a commoning movement, though not necessarily yet at scaled up, more polycentric levels. Still, I am confident this scaling up will happen, and will do so through networking around local actions. One of the lessons from the Finger Lakes initiative is the importance of keeping decision-making alive at the local level where people are implicated in local versions of what's at stake at a larger, more global level. They can gain confidence in their own agency (as change agents) through the local policy making and actions they take part in.

Imagine yourself as one of these implicated participants in healing our relations with each other and with the living world.

Glossary

anam cara — a soul friend, an equal who is at the same time devoted to calling out the best in another, bending and shaping self and self-interest toward right relations, community and the common good.

baile — a tenancy subject to rent, which for centuries took an in-kind form as so many "stones" of cheese, bales of wool, bushels of grain and lambs for slaughter.

bothy — a small stone hut used mostly as sleeping quarters.

byre — a cow shed. Traditionally, it was attached to one end of a long-house-style cottage, sharing the same roof, and accessed from inside, often from the kitchen or pantry, and was used to house livestock, including ducks and chickens.

commodity — originally a personal benefit or advantage.

common — derived from the Latin *com* (together) and *unus* (one); hence, together-as-one. Also from the Latin *com* and *munis* (obligation); hence "together in obligation."

a common(s) — a self-governing community of people who inhabit or share the use of land; a habitat of mutual interrelationships that includes community and land shared in common, often including fields, pastureland, fens and forests. The term is often used to refer to the land itself, such as a grazing common, a village common.

commoning — to share, to commune, to do things in shares, including by pooling resources, and by extension, to decide things together. In premodern times, it was a way of life, a particular way of weaving the threads of daily life, the how of things with the why to give meaning and a sense of what's real and relevant.

common knowledge — as a verb, to share knowledge, especially drawn from direct experience, to pool it in some shared interest; as a noun, knowledge gleaned by insiders as insiders, participants alive to an action or situation in which they're involved. See also knowledge commons.

common of estover — the right to take wood from the forest or waste land to repair gates or farm equipment.

commons consciousness — a consciousness that extends the sense of self into a web of mutual relations with others and land in a shared habitat, and which develops through ongoing commons practices. See also ethos of the commons.

credit — originally a quality of one's character, specifically a quality of neighborliness; someone who could be counted to assist, who returned good will for good will.

crux cottage — a traditional form of housing associated with premodern Scotland, featuring a set of crossed timbers at either end of the longhouse bungalow which, anchored in the ground, carried the weight of the roof, rather than having it rest on the walls.

customary economy — historical premodern economy centered in community relations and the land. Sometimes called "moral economy," though this term has lost favor, as romanticizing and idealizing.

drifter — a field officer who kept count of livestock.

driftway — a common right-of-way through others' lands; an old pathway which also served as a common right-of-way.

dualchas — see duthchas.

duthaich — ancestral homelands.

duthchas — a lived set of rights and also responsibilities toward one's family and the land that they inhabited.

ethos of the commons — a feeling for sharing and contributing to the well-being of community and shared habitat and, by extension, of the Earth, through shared engagement with it. See also commons consciousness.

fermtoun — a commons farming township, hamlet or village. In premodern times, it was the smallest social unit of the day, with its resident community often derived from earlier seminomadic bands and tribes.

feu charter — a charter bestowing control of land, given by kings to loyal barons and lords as a sort of local franchise of control.

flitting — the major annual trek from fermtoun settlements to the upland common pasture, with almost the entire community, along with their livestock, taking part in this summer relocation.

herd — a field officer who kept animals on track.

implicated participant — a term, drawn from the work of time theorist Barbara Adam, to designate a way of being in time, namely present, ready to take part in and share responsibility for what's going on.

knowledge commons — a database or other collection of knowledge that's being shared (e.g. articles, reports, stories) and/or a platform to develop and extend knowledge online and off. See also common knowledge.

lex loci — the customary premodern local jurisdiction of law and justice.

loan — a common right-of-way through others' lands.

mark stone — a large, often standing stone used to mark the boundaries of land that was farmed in common.

nabec — (meaning "neighborliness") seasonal meeting of the fermtoun common.

naire — the capacity to know what is wrong and right.

peregrini — pilgrims and Jesus movement followers who fanned out from the Middle East spreading word of Christ's message and who arrived in Scotland in the 4th century CE.

pinfold — a pound where errant animals were kept.

piscary — the right to fish.

poindler — see pounder.

pounder — a local constable responsible for ensuring that the stints were honored and authorized to impound any cattle or sheep that broke this or other commons bylaws or regulations.

property — originally a characteristic and also a right to something, a claim; through John Locke a capacity for self-improvement, the democratic birthright of all. Locke argued, therefore, that everyone was free to use the property vested in their own talents and labor to improve their lot and advance their own self-interest.

public house — a venue for commons and other public meetings — the origin of the modern word "pub."

rack renting — A term that describes an extremely high or extortionate rent. Derived from to rack, meaning to stretch, including to be tortured by being stretched on a rack.

res communi — things that cannot be privately owned because they are meant to sustain everyone.

res divini juris — things that cannot be privately owned because they are imbued with the sacred, the divine.

right relations — mutual recognition and respect toward both other people and other lifeforms.

shieling — upland common pasture and any simple stone buildings erected there, the word originally meaning "enclosure in the wilderness."

stint — one of the self-governing powers exercised by local commons; a limit on something, such as the number of sheep and cattle to be sent to the shieling pasture, intended as a conservation measure to ensure the sustainability of, in this case, the pasture.

township — see fermtoun.

tuatha — the people.

turbury — the right to cut peat or turf for fuel.

Endnotes

Introduction

1. Since beginning this book, I have come to see the seemingly appealing term "settler" in new light, since my people "settled" on often unceded ancestral lands of Canada's Indigenous peoples. I now acknowledge that they participated in appropriating this land, as their ancestral lands had been similarly appropriated in Scotland.
2. See Arundhati Roy. "Confronting Empire." Porto Alegre, Brazil, January 27, 2003. [online]. [cited October 29, 2013]. ratical.org/ratville/CAH/AR012703.html.

Chapter 1: At an Impasse

1. Robert Romanyshyn. *Technology as Symptom and Dream*. Routledge, 1989.
2. Richard Louv. *Last Child in the Woods: Saving Our Children From Nature-Deficit Disorder*. Algonquin, 2008.
3. William Christian & Sheila Grant, eds. *The George Grant Reader*. University of Toronto, 1998, p. 452.
4. George Grant. *Technology and Empire: Perspectives on North America*. Anansi, 1969, pp. 16 and 32.

Chapter 2: Crossing a Threshold

1. Alasdair MacMhaoirn, Personal Communication, February 5, 2013.

2. T.M. Devine. *Clanship to Crofters' War: The social transformation of the Scottish Highlands.* Manchester University, 1994, p. 33.

3. Thomas Johnston. *The History of the Working Class in Scotland.* Forward, 1929, p. 155.

4. Ibid.

5. Elizabeth Foyster and Christopher A. Whatley, eds. *A History of Everyday Life in Scotland, 1600–1800.* Edinburgh University, 2010, p. 3.

6. Jeanette Neeson. *Commoners: Common Right, Enclosure and Social Change in England, 1700–1820.* Cambridge, 1996, p. 5.

7. Rosemary Gibson. *The Scottish Countryside: Its Changing Face, 1700–2000.* John Donald, 1976, p. 52.

Chapter 3: To the Shieling

1. Albert Bil. *The Shieling 1600–1840: The Case of the Central Scottish Highlands.* John Donald, 1990, p. 183.

2. Neeson, p. 320.

3. Nicholas Blomley. "Making Private Property: Enclosure, Common Right and the Work of Hedges." *Rural History,* Vol. 18#1 (2007), p. 15.

4. Michael Newton. *Warriors of the Word: The World of the Scottish Highlanders.* Birlinn, 2009, p. 287.

5. Ibid., p. 300.

6. Heather Menzies. "When Roots Grow Back into the Earth" in David R. Boyd, ed. *Northern Wild: Best Contemporary Canadian Nature Writing.* Greystone, 2001, pp. 167–175.

7. R.L. Cann et al. "Mitochondrial DNA and human evolution." *Nature* Vol. 385 (January 1, 1987), pp. 31–6.

Chapter 4: A Field in Good Heart

1. Rev. Archibald Menzies. *The Statistical Account of Scotland, Vol. XII, 1791–1799.* E.P. Publishing Ltd., 1977, p. 300.

2. Neeson, p. 132.

3. Johnston, p. 156.

4. See Ken Wilber, ed. *Quantum Questions: Mystical Writings of the World's Greatest Physicists.* First Print, 1984; Fritjof Capra. *The Turning Point: Science, Society, and the Rising Culture.* Simon & Schuster, 1982; Fritjof Capra. *The Tao of Physics: An Exploration of the Parallels between Modern Physics and Eastern Mysticism.* Wildwood House, 1975.

Chapter 5: *Duthchas* and the Ethos of the Commons

1. Newton, p. 306.
2. Alasdair MacMhaoirn. Personal Communication, February 5, 2013.
3. Johnston, p.158.
4. Andy Wightman. *The Poor Had No Lawyers: Who Owns Scotland (And How They Got It)*. Birlinn, 2010, pg. 23.
5. Devine, p. 33.
6. Newton, p. 145.
7. *The Compact Edition of the Oxford English Dictionary*, Vol. 1. Oxford, 1971, s.v. "common.". See common in glossary.
8. Newton, p. 306.
9. Irene M. Spry. "The Tragedy of the Loss of the Commons" in Ian A.L. Getty and Antoine S. Lussier, eds. *As Long as the Sun Shines and the Water Flows: A Reader in Canadian Native Studies*. University of British Columbia, 1983, pp. 203–228.
10. Lewis Hyde. *Common as Air: Revolution, Art, and Ownership*. Farrar, Straus and Giroux, 2010, p. 173.
11. David Cowan & Chris Arnold. *Ley lines and Earth Energies*. Adventures Unlimited Press, 2003, p.82)
12. Newton, p. 130.
13. Nick Walker. "Mapping traditional place names in Canada's North." *Canadian Geographic*, July/August 2013. [online]. [cited September 20, 2013]. canadiangeographic.ca/magazine/ja13/inuit_heritage_trust.asp.

Chapter 6: Coming Home to the Sacred

1. David Prentice Menzies. *The Red & White Book of Menzies*. Bank & Co., 1894, p. 114.
2. Newton, p. 321.
3. Ibid., pp. 323–4.
4. Morris Neyelle, Personal Communication, August 8, 2013.
5. I've drawn on a number of sources here, including Robert O'Driscoll, ed. *The Celtic Consciousness*. George Braziller, 1981; Ian Bradley. *Celtic Christianity: Making Myths and Chasing Dreams*. Edinburgh, 1999.
6. Newton, p. 217.
7. Mary Low. *Celtic Christianity and Nature: Early Irish and Hebridean Traditions*. Edinburgh, 1997, p. 78.

8. Ibid., p. 117.

9. Frank Delaney. *The Celts*. Harper Collins, 1989, p. 89.

10. Alexander Carmichael. *Carmina Gadelica: Hymns & Incantations*. Floris, 1994, p. 345.

11. J. Philip Newell. *Christ of the Celts: The Healing of Creation*. Wild Goose Publications, 2008, p. 31.

12. Keith Wrightson. *Earthly Necessities: Economic Lives in Early Modern Britain*. Yale, 2002, p. 78.

13. Mary C. Earle. *Celtic Christian Spirituality: Essential Writings — Annotated & Explained*. Skylight Illuminations, 2011, p. 103.

14. E. Richard Atleo. *Principles of Tsawalk: An Indigenous Approach to Global Crisis*. University of British Columbia, 2011, pp. 127 and 84.

15. Newton, pp. 129 and 157.

16. Ibid., p. 148.

17. Atleo, p. 117.

18. Irene M. Spry. *From the Hunt to the Homestead*. Unpublished Manuscript available in Spry papers at National Archives of Canada. The references for this statement include Hugh A. Dempsey. *Crowfoot: Chief of the Blackfeet*. Hurtig, 1972, pp. 5, 62 and 65.

19. John Raulston Saul. *A Fair Country: Telling Truths About Canada*. Viking, 2008, p. 51.

20. Ibid., p. 124.

21. Devine, p. 6.

Chapter 7: The Tragedy of the Commons Revisited

1. Susan Jane Buck Cox. "No tragedy on the commons." *Environmental Ethics* Vol. 7#1 (1985), pp. 49–61.

2. Garrett Hardin."The Tragedy of the Commons." *Science* Vol. 162#3859 (December 13, 1968), pp. 1243–1248. [online]. [cited September 21, 2013]. garretthardinsociety.org/articles/art_tragedy_of_the_commons.html.

3. W. F. Lloyd. *Two Lectures on the Checks to Population*. Oxford, 1833 reprinted (in part) in G. Hardin, ed. *Population, Evolution, and Birth Control: A Collage of Controversial Ideas*. Freeman, 1964, p. 37.

4. The details here are from many sources, principally Alexander Fenton. *Scottish Country Life*. John Donald, 1976; Bil. *The Shieling* and Devine. *Clanship to Crofters' War*.

5. Johnston, p. 156.
6. E.P. Thompson. *Customs in Common: Studies in Traditional Popular Culture*. New Press, 1993, pp. 4 and 144.
7. Karl Polanyi. *The Great Transformation*. Beacon, 1957; Wrightson.
8. W.E. Tate. *The English Village Community and the Enclosure Movements*. Gollancz, 1967, frontispiece.
9. Dodgshon quoted in Elizabeth Foyster and Christopher A. Whatle, eds. *A History of Everyday Life in Scotland, 1600–1800*. Edinburgh, 2010, p. 45.
10. Nicholas K. Blomley. *Law, Space and the Geographies of Power*. Guilford, 1994, pp. 69–105.
11. Neeson, p. 163.
12. Carolyn Merchant. *The Death of Nature: Women, Ecology and the Scientific Revolution*. Harper & Row, 1980, p. 171.)
13. Tate, p. 161.
14. Neeson, p. 284.
15. Tate, p. 148.
16. Thompson, p. 165.

Chapter 8: Feudal Land Charters and Private Property

1. Johnston, p. 19.
2. Bil, p. 80.
3. Devine, p. 33.
4. Wightman, p. 46.
5. Devine, pp. 41 and 44.
6. Thompson, p. 161.
7. Ibid., p. 160.
8. Ibid., p. 164.
9. Ibid., p. 135.
10. Ibid., p. 162.

Chapter 9: The Real Tragedy of the Loss of the Commons

1. Elinor Ostrom. *Governing the Commons: The Evolution of Institutions for Collective Action*. Cambridge, 1990.
2. Neeson, p. 45. The Clearances (with a capital C) refers to the forced removal of long-standing inhabitants of lands and villages through a combination of legal maneuvers such as enclosure petitions and economic ones like charging exorbitant rent for land people had traditionally

occupied through tenancies. There were two waves of this, one in the mid-18th century and the second, in the early decades of the 19th century.

3. Tate, p. 155.

4. John Clark, ed. *Renewing the Earth: The Promise of Social Ecology.* Green Print, 1990, p. 94.

5. Williams, p. 102.

6. Tate, p. 31.

7. Wightman, p. 42.

8. Wrightson, p. 78.

9. Ibid., p. 74.

10. Neeson, p. 154.

11. Mark Abley. *Spoken Here: Travels Among Threatened Languages.* Houghton-Mifflin, 2003, p. 17.

12. Hyde, p. 171.

Chapter 10: From Premodern Past to Digital Present

1. Maude Barlow. *Blue Future: Protecting Water for People and the Planet Forever.* Anansi, 2013, pp. 251 and 104.

2. Polanyi, pp. 42 and 57.

3. Ostrom. *Governing the Commons.*

4. See Capra, *The Tao of Physics*; Wilber, *Quantum Questions.*

5. Joanna Macy. *Coming Back to Life: Practices to Reconnect Our Lives, Our World.* New Society, 1998, pp. 21 and 23.

6. David C. Korten. *The Great Turning: From Empire to Earth Community.* Kumarian, 2006, pp. 20 and 21.

7. Barbara Adam. *Timewatch: The Social Analysis of Time.* Polity Press, 1995, p. 145.

8. Ibid., p. 157.

9. See Chapter 7, "Children's Time and Attention Deficit Disorder" in Heather Menzies. *No Time: Stress and the Crisis of Modern Life.* Douglas & McIntyre, 2005.

Chapter 11: Reclaiming the Commons on Gabriola Island

1. P. Routledge. "Activist Geographies" in R. Kitchin and N. Thrift, eds. *International Encyclopedia of Human Geography*, Vol. 1. Elsevier, 2009, p. 7.

2. Jan L. Flora. "Social Capital and Communities of Place." *Rural Sociology* Vol. 63#4 (December 1998), p. 482.

3. Vincent Ostrom. "Polycentricity." Working paper, 1972. [online]. [cited December 13, 2013]. hdl.handle.net/10535/3763; Richard E. Wagner. "Self-governance, polycentrism and federalism: recurring themes in Vincent Ostrom's scholarly oeuvre." *Journal of Economic Behavior & Organization*, Vol. 57#2 (June 2005), pp. 173–188.

4. Text is available on the website: gabriolacommons.ca/pdf/covenant-dr2.pdf.

5. The Gabriola Commons. [online]. [cited September 10, 2013]. gabriolacommons.ca/index.html.

6. Benedict Anderson. *Imagined Communities: Reflections on the Origin and Spread of Nationalism*. Verso, 1983, p. 16.

7. Judith Roux, Personal Communication, December 9, 2013.

8. Ibid.

Chapter 12: Capacity Building #1 — Healing and Connecting with Our Selves

1. *Compact Oxford English Dictionary*, s.v. "common (n.)" and "common (v.)." See Glossary at end of book.

2. Elizabeth Renzetti. "Loneliness: the Trouble with Solitude." *The Globe and Mail*, November 23, 2013, p. F1.

3. Keith O'Brien. "The Empathy Deficit." *Boston Globe*, October 17, 2010. [online]. [cited December 3, 2013]. boston.com/bostonglobe/ideas/articles/2010/10/17/the_empathy_deficit/.

4. Sherry Turkle. *Alone Together: Why We Expect More from Technology and Less from Each Other*. Basic, 2011, p. 168.

5. Kate Lunau. "The Broken Generation." *Maclean's Magazine*, September 10, 2012, p. 56.

6. Bruce Alexander. *The Globalization of Addiction: A Study in Poverty of the Spirit*. Oxford, 2008.

7. Gabor Maté. *In the Realm of the Hungry Ghosts: Close Encounters with Addiction*. Knopf, 2008, p. 185. See also Menzies, *No Time*, pp. 165–70.

8. Menzies, *No Time*, pp. 140–157.

Chapter 13: Capacity Building # 2 — Healing, Habitats and Reconnecting with Nature

1. Richard C. Lewontin. *Biology as Ideology: The Doctrine of DNA*. Anansi, 1991, p. 83.

2. Maté, p 183.

3. Ibid., pp.185–8.

4. Frank R. Wilson. *The Hand: How Its Use Shapes the Brain, Language, and Human Culture* quoted in Louv, p. 67.

5. Theodore Roszak. *The Voice of the Earth* quoted in Louv, p. 44.

6. See Part I in Louv.

7. Menzies, *No Time*, p. 167.

8. Turkle, p. 295.

9. Ibid., p. 280 n. 341.

10. Lunau, "The Broken Generation."

11. Turkle, p. 179.

12. Marshall McLuhan (with Quentin Fiore). *The Medium is the Massage: An Inventory of Effects*. Bantam, 1967, p. 26. See also Marshall McLuhan. *Understanding Media: The Extensions of Man*. MIT, 1999.

13. William Bryant Logan. *Dirt: The Ecstatic Skin of the Earth*. Riverhead, 1995.

Chapter 14: Capacity Building # 3 — Ecoliteracy and Knowing through Implicated Participation

1. Boaventura de Sousa Santos. "The World Social Forum: Toward a Counter-Hegemonic Globalisation" in Jai Sen and Peter Waterman, eds. *World Social Forum: Challenging Empires*. Black Rose, 2009, p. 194.

2. Tim Ingold. *The Perception of the Environment: Essays on Livelihood, Dwelling and Skill*. Routledge, 2000.

3. Ibid, p. 39.

4. I am indebted to Irene Guijt, PhD for this nuanced understanding. Irene Guijt, Personal Communication, November 25, 2013.

5. Ingold, p. 47.

6. Bill McKibben. "Global Warming's Terrifying New Math." Comment in *Rolling Stone Magazine*, August 2, 2012; William D. Nordhaus. *The Climate Casino: Risk, Uncertainty and Economics for a Warming World*. Yale, 2013.

7. Marilynne Robinson. *Absence of Mind: The Dispelling of Inwardness from the Modern Myth of the Self*. Yale, 2010, pp. 59 and 60.

8. Evelyn Fox Keller. *A Feeling for the Organism: The Life and Work of Barbara McClintock*. Freeman, 1983.

9. Peggy Tripp and Linda Muzzin, eds. *Teaching as Activism: Equity Meets Environmentalism*. McGill-Queens, 2005, pp. 25–33.

10. J.K. Gibson-Graham. *A Postcapitalist Politics*. University of Minnesota, 2006, p. xxiii.

11. Ingold, p. 417.

12. Manitoba Education. "What is Ecological Literacy?" Draft Global Issues Pilot August 2011. [online]. [cited November 13, 2013]. edu.gov.mb.ca/k12/cur/socstud/global_issues/ecological_literacy.pdf. See also Center for Ecoliteracy website. [online]. [cited November 13, 2013]. ecoliteracy.org.

Chapter 15: Capacity Building #4 — Commoning Knowledge and Knowledge Commons

1. Heather Menzies. *By the Labour of their Hands: The Story of Ontario Cheddar Cheese*. Quarry, 1994, p. 25.

2. Personal note: Terms like "settler" and "homesteading in the bush" have become problematic to me as I've worked on this book. The land was not "bush" to be "settled" when it was home to Canada's first peoples, including the Huron, Ojibwe and others displaced by these homesteading newcomers.

3. Walter Riddell. *The Riddell Papers*, Ontario Archives excerpted in Menzies, *By the Labour*, p. 243.

4. Menzies, *By the Labour*, chapter on "Bush Farming, Bees and Agricultural Societies." This information was drawn from numerous sources, including Phillip Dodds. *The Story of Agricultural Fairs and Exhibitions 1792–1967*. Picton Gazette Publishing, 1967.

5. Menzies, *By the Labour*, p. 25.

6. F.L. Dickinson. *Prairie Wheat: Three Centuries of Wheat Varieties in Western Canada*. The Canada Grain Council, n.d.

7. Menzies, *By the Labour*, p. 11.

8. Guijt, Personal Communication.

9. John Gaventa and Felix Bivens. "Co-constructing Democratic Knowledge for Social Justice: Lessons from an International Research Collaboration" in *Social Justice and the University: Globalization, Human Rights, and the Future of Democracy*. Palgrave MacMillan (Scholarly Division), 2014.

10. David Geoffrey Smith, Personal Communication, 28 November 2013. See also his "Wisdom Responses to Globalization: The Pedagogic Context" in W. Pinar, ed. *The International Handbook of Curriculum Research*, 2nd ed. Routledge, 2013.

11. Ingold, p. 411.

12. Thomas R. Berger. *Northern Frontier, Northern Homeland: The Report of the Mackenzie Valley Pipeline Inquiry, Volume One.* Minister of Supply and Services Canada, 1977. [online]. [cited November 14, 2013]. yukondigitallibrary.ca/digitalbook/northernfrontiersocialimpactenvironmentalimpact/.

Chapter 16: Capacity Building # 5 — Commons Organizing and the Common Good

1. Mairi Robinson, ed-in-chief. *Concise Scots Dictionary.* Polygon, 1985, p. 109.
2. Wrightson, pp. 115 (raiemement) and 150.
3. Excerpts quoted in Tate, p. 65. See also Thomas More. *Utopia.* Cambridge, 1989, pp. 18–19.
4. Oliver Goldsmith. "The Deserted Village." [online]. [cited September 12, 2013]. poetryfoundation.org/poem/173557.
5. Tony Judt. *Ill Fares the Land.* Penguin, 2010, pp. 96, 180 and 193.
6. Ibid., p. 188.
7. Naomi Klein. "Reclaiming the Commons." *New Left Review* #9 (May/June 2001), p. 88.
8. Elinor Ostrom. "The Future of the Commons: Beyond Market Failure and Government Regulation" in Institute of Economic Affairs. *The Future of the Commons.* IEA, 2012, pp 69–70. [online]. [cited November 15, 2013]. iea.org.uk/sites/default/files/publications/files/IEA Future of the Commons web 29-1.10.12.pdf.
9. Spry, *From the Hunt to the Homestead*, p. 285. See also Diamond Jenness. *Indians of Canada*, 7th ed. University of Toronto, 1978, Chapter IX.
10. Angus J.L. Winchester. *The Harvest of the Hills: Rural Life in Northern England and the Scottish Borders, 1400–1700.* Edinburgh, 2000, p. 83.
11. Margaret A. McKean. "Management of Traditional Common Lands (*Iriachi*) in Japan" in National Research Council (US). *Proceedings of the Conference on Common Property Resource Management.* National Academy Press, 1986, p. 534.
12. Bill McKibben. *Deep Economy: The Wealth of Communities and the Durable Future.* St. Martin's Griffin, 2007; *Eaarth: Making a Life on a Tough New Planet.* Times, 2010.
13. Mark Kingwell. *Unruly Voices: Essays on Democracy, Civility & the Human Imagination.* Biblioasis, 2012.

14. Robert Putnam. *Bowling Alone: The Collapse and Revival of American Community*. Simon & Schuster, 2000, p. 23.
15. Mark Kingwell. *A Civil Tongue: Justice, Dialogue, and the Politics of Pluralism*. Pennsylvania State, 1995, p. 120.
16. Robert Bierstedt quoted in Severyn T. Bruyn. "Beyond the Market and the State" in Severyn T. Bruyn and James Meehan, eds. *Beyond the Market and the State: New Directions in Community Development*. Temple, 1987, p. 14.
17. Fred Azcarate quoted in Judy Rebick. "Another U.S. Is Happening" in Sen and Waterman, *World Social Forum*, p. 306.
18. Ibid., pp 305–314.

Chapter 17: Capacity Building #6 — A Spirit Dialogue, Reconnecting with Creation

1. Quintin Hoare and Geoffrey Nowell Smith, eds. Antonio Gramsci. *Selections from Prison Notebooks*. International, 1971, pp. 419–25.
2. Edith Rodgers. *Discussion of Holidays in the Later Middle Ages*. AMS Press, 1967.
3. Richard Rohr. *A Lever and a Place to Stand: The Contemplative Stance, the Active Prayer*. Hidden Spring, 2011, p. 59.
4. Ibid., p. 26
5. Rochelle Graham, Flora Litt and Wayne Irwin. *Healing from the Heart: A Guide to Christian Healing for Individuals and Groups*. WoodLake, 2008, p. 16.
6. Ibid.
7. Ibid., p. 23.
8. Community Iona. *Iona Abbey Worship Book*. Wild Goose, 2001, p. 51.
9. Truth and Reconciliation Commission of Canada. "About Us." [online]. [cited November 15, 2013]. trc.ca/websites/trcinstitution/index.php?p=4.
10. These quotes are from the notes I took at the time.
11. Matthew Fox. *Original Blessing: A Primer in Creation Spirituality Presented in Four Paths, Twenty-Six Themes, and Two Questions*. Bear and Company, 1983, p. 11.
12. Rita Nakashima Brock and Rebecca Ann Parker. *Saving Paradise: How Christianity Traded Love of This World for Crucifixion and Empire*. Beacon, 2008, p. 72.
13. Fox, p. 11.

14. Brock and Parker, p. 106.

15. Barlow, p. 135.

16. Pat Mayberry. "Called by Earth and Sky (Du Ciel et de la terre)" in *More Voices. Supplement to Voices United: The Hymn and Worship Book of the United Church of Canada*. United Church Publishing House, 2007, p. 135.

17. Thomas Berry. *The Dream of the Earth*. Sierra Club, 1988, p. 93.

Chapter 18: An Historical Frame for Current Activism

1. *Compact Oxford English Dictionary*, s.v. "manifesto."

2. Nicholas Blomley. "Enclosure, Common Right and the Property of the Poor." *Social & Legal Studies*, Vol. 17 (2008), p. 311. [online]. [cited November 25, 2013]. sls.sagepub.com/cgi/content/abstract/17/3/311.

3. Brewster Kneen. "Redefining 'property': Private Property, the Commons and the Public Domain." *Seedling*, January 2004, p. 5. [online]. [cited December 5, 2013]. grain.org/article/archive/categories/39-seedling-january-2004.

4. Naomi Klein. *Fences and Windows: Dispatches from the Front Lines of the Globalization Debate*. Picador, 2002, p. 222–3.

5. Heather Menzies. *Whose Brave New World? the information highway and the new economy*. Between the Lines, 1996, p. 161.

6. Karl Marx and Frederick Engels. *The Communist Manifesto: A Modern Edition*. Verso, 2012; Walter Young. *Anatomy of a Party: The National CCF 1932–61*. University of Toronto, 1969, pp. 304–313; Front de Libération du Québec. Manifesto of October 1970. [online]. [cited November 25, 2013]. marxists.org/history/canada/quebec/flq/1970/manifesto.htm; Sen and Waterman, pp. 238–41.

Chapter 19: Some Personal Acts of Reconnection

1. Jane's Walk website. [online]. [cited October 16, 2013]. janeswalk.org.

2. Jonathan Rowe, ed. Peter Barnes. *Our Common Wealth: The Hidden Economy That Makes Everything Else Work*. Berrett-Koehler, 2013, p. 94.

3. Carp Ridge Learning Centre. *Ridgewoods Outdoor Programs*. [online]. [cited November 25, 2013]. carpridgelearningcentre.ca/preschool.html.

4. Children & Nature Network website. [online]. [cited October 16, 2013]. childrenandnature.org.

5. National Trust website. [online]. [cited October 16, 2013]. nationaltrust.org.uk.

6. Cranedale Centre website. [online]. [cited December 13, 2013]. cranedale.com.

7. The Field Studies Council website. [online]. [cited October 16, 2013]. field-studies-council.org.

8. Open Air Laboratories website. [online]. [cited October 16, 2013]. opalexplorenature.org.

9. Vancouver Rape Relief and Women's Shelter. *Fleshmapping: Vancouver Markets Pacific Women*, 2008. [online]. [cited December 14, 2013]. rapereliefshelter.bc.ca/fleshmapping-vancouver-markets-pacific-women-2008.

10. The Edible Bus Stop webpage. [online]. [cited October 17, 2013]. theediblebusstop.org.

11. Mundraub website. [online]. [cited October 17, 2013]. mundraub.org.

12. Dan Rubinstein. "How natives find power in a long-distance walk." *The Globe and Mail,*. May 11, 2013, p. F5.

13. Abraham Bearskin, Personal Communication, October 8, 2013.

14. Rubinstein, "How natives find power."

Chapter 20: Gardening, Agroecology and Forming Relationships with the Land

1. K. Prager and F. Vanclay. "Landcare in Australia and Germany: comparing structure and policies for community engagement in natural resource management." *Ecological Management and Restoration*, Vol. 11#3 (2010), pp. 187–93.

2. Ray Ford. "Death and rebirth on the Don River." *Canadian Geographic*, June, 2011. [online]. [cited November 26, 2013]. canadiangeographic.ca/magazine/jun11/don_river_watershed.asp.

3. Riverkeeper website. [online]. [cited November 26, 2013]. riverkeeper.org.

4. Terry Hartig. "Green space, psychological restoration and health inequality." *The Lancet*, Vol. 372#9650 (November 8, 2008), pp. 1614–1615; Homewood website. [online]. [cited December 5, 2013]. Homewood.org/programs-and-services/therapies. [cited]

5. Peter Butter, Personal Communication, July 10, 2013.

6. Kate Hammer. "From seedlings sprout teachable moments." *The Globe and Mail*. May 5, 2012, p. A11.

7. UBC Farm. *Children's Learning Garden*. [online]. [cited November 20, 2013.] ubcfarm.ubc.ca/teaching-learning/childrens-learning-garden/.

8. Hammer, "From seedlings."

9. Dickson Despommier. *The Vertical Farm: Feeding the World in the 21st Century*. Thomas Dunne, 2010.

10. Kevin Spurgaitis. "Global Crisis, Urban Answers." *The United Church Observer*, July/August 2012, p. 31.

11. Kathryn Colasanti et al. "Growing food in the city: the Production potential of Detroit's vacant land." C.S. Mott Group for Sustainable Food Systems, Michigan State University, June 2010; Tavia Grant. "Won't Stop Believing." *The Globe and Mail*, August 31, 2013, pp. F6–7.

12. Nick Saul and Andrea Curtis. *The Stop. How the Fight for Good Food Transformed a Community and Inspired a Movement*. Random House, 2013.

13. Peggy Cameron, Friends of Halifax Common, Personal Communication, June 14, 2013; Friends of the Halifax Common website. [online]. [cited September 24, 2013]. halifaxcommon.ca.

14. Halifax Garden Network website. [online]. [cited October 18, 2013]. halifaxgardennetwork.wordpress.com/2012/07/03/welcome-common-roots-urban-farm/.

15. Food Secure Canada. *Resetting the Table — A People's Food Policy for Canada*. [online]. [cited November 26, 2013]. foodsecurecanada.org/policy-advocacy/resetting-table.

16. Chris Bisson. "Forests for the People: Resisting Neoliberalism Through Permaculture Design." MA thesis, Carleton University, 2013.

17. Stephen R. Gliessman. *Agroecology: The Ecology of Sustainable Food Systems*, 2nd ed. CRC Press, 2007, pp. 23 and 19.

18. Helke Ferrie. "Biotech Losing Ground: Evidence Grows of harmful effects of GMOs on human health." *CCPA Monitor*, October 2011, p. 13.

19. Luiza Ch. Savage, "End of the Line," in *Maclean's Magazine*. Feb. 3, 2014, p. 26.

20. Alastair Iles and Robin Marsh. "Nurturing Diversified Farming Systems in Industrialized Countries: How Public Policy Can Contribute." *Ecology and Society*, Vol. 17#4, p. 6.

21. Ibid., p. 3 and 2.

22. Ibid., p. 12.

Chapter 21: An Economy of Fair Trade and Right Relations

1. International Labor Rights Forum. "One Year After Fire, ILRF Urges Brands to Accept Responsibility." [online]. [cited November 27, 2013]. laborrights.org.

2. Bill Hynd and Carol Miller. "Oxfam Canada: The 'Fair Trade in Coffee' Campaign" in Elizabeth Whitmore, Maureen G. Wilson and Avery Calhoun, eds. *Activism That Works*. Fernwood, 2011, pp. 29–43.
3. Wrightson, p. 111.
4. A.J. Dellinger. 'Buycott' App review in *Digitaltrends.com*. [online]. [cited May 25, 2013].
5. Iles and Marsh, p. 11.
6. Ibid.
7. Graciela Watrous. "The Promise of For-Profit Urban Agriculture." *The Stanford Daily*, May 9, 2013. [online]. [cited November 27, 2013]. stanforddaily.com/2013/05/09/the-promise-of-for-profit-urban-agriculture/.
8. Community Food Centres Canada website. [online]. [cited October 21, 2013]. cfccanada.ca.
9. Sarah Elton. "Can a locavore dream of public produce come true?" *The Globe and Mail*, July 7, 2012, pp. F1 and F7.
10. Gloria L. Gallardo Fernandez and Eva Friman. "Capable Leadership, Institutional Skills and Resource Abundance Behind Flourishing Coastal Marine Commons in Chile" in David Bollier and Silke Helfrich, eds. *The Wealth of the Commons: A World Beyond Market and State*. Levellers, 2012, pp. 258–263.
11. Gibson-Graham, pp. 188-9; see also Nuestras Raices website. [online]. [cited November 20, 2013). nuestras-raices.org.
12. Farmer's Markets Association of Manitoba Co-op Inc. website. [online]. [cited November 29, 2013]. fmam.ca.
13. Le Centre Haïtien du Leadership et de l'Excellence and the Coady International Institute. *If Change Should Come, We Should Bring It: Stories of Citizen-led Development in Haiti*. Coady Institute, 2013. [online]. [cited November 27, 2013].coady.stfx.ca/tinroom/assets/file/If_Change_should_come.pdf.
14. Judy Rebick. *Transforming Power: From the Personal to the Political*. Penguin, 2009, p. 44.
15. Nora Loreto. *From Demonized to Organized: Building the New Union Movement*. Canadian Centre for Policy Alternatives, 2013, p. 162.)
16. Unpublished paper sent to author by Lydia Warkentin. Personal Communication, November 22, 2013.

17. Amy Frye, Personal Communication, November 17, 2013.
18. Loreto, p. 164.
19. "2012 International Summit of Cooperatives." An Information Feature in *The Globe and Mail*, October 5, 2012.
20. Christa Muller. "Practicing Commons in Community Gardens: Urban Gardening as a Corrective for Homo Economicus" in Bollier and Helfrich, p. 221.

Chapter 22: Common Knowledge and Knowledge Commons

1. Gibson-Graham, p. 8.
2. Dorothy E. Smith. *The Conceptual Practices of Power: A Feminist Sociology of Knowledge*. University of Toronto, 1990.
3. Tom Marcantonio, Personal Communication, October 2, 2013.
4. Opalexplorenature. *Water Survey*. [online]. [cited October 22, 2013]. opalexplorenature.org/WaterSurvey.
5. Bee Haven International website. [online]. [cited Octrober 22, 2013]. beehaveninternational.org.
6. Water-Research.net website. [online]. [cited October 22, 2013]. water-research.net.
7. Trisha Gura. "Citizen science: Amateur experts." *Nature* Vol. 496 (April 11, 2013), pp. 259–61.
8. Amy Freitag, Max J. Pfeffer. "Process, Not Product: Investigating Recommendations for Improving Citizen Science 'Success.'" *PLoS One* Vol 8#5 (May 15, 2013). [online]. [cited November 28, 2013]. plosone.org/article/info:doi/10.1371/journal.pone.0064079.
9. Iles and Marsh, pp. 10, 6 and 3.
10. Patrick Kerans. *A Pessimist's Hope: Food and the Ecological Crisis*. Baico Publishing, 2011, pp.147-9.
11. Global Alliance on Community-Engaged Research website. gacer.org; Development Research Centre on Citizenship, Participation and Accountability website. drc-citizenship.org. Both cites: [online]. [cited October 22, 2013].
12. Gaventa and Bivens.
13. Ibid.
14. Frank Adams. *Unearthing Seeds of Fire: The Idea of Highlander*. John F. Blair Publishing, 1980, p. 121.

15. Brianne Peters. "Learning Together to Promote Citizen-led Development." Coady International Institute. [online]. [cited November 28, 2013]. aucc.ca/wp-content/uploads/2013/07/learning-together-to-promote-citizen-led-development-st-francis-xavier-idrc-case-study-2013.pdf.

16. Graham Longfor, Andrew Clement, Michael Gurstein and Leslie Regan Shade. "Connecting Canadians? Community Informatics Perspectives on Community Networking Initiatives" in Andrew Clement et al, eds. *Connecting Canadians: Investigations in Community Informatics*. Athabasca, 2012, pp. 5–7.

17. International Association for the Study of the Commons website. [online]. [cited October 22, 2013]. iasc-commons.org.

18. Creative Commons website. [online]. [cited October 22, 2013]. creativecommons.org.

19. The POD knowledge exchange website. [online]. [cited November 29, 2013]. thepod.cfccanada.ca.

20. "Chapter Activist Profile: Mary McCandless, Winnipeg, Manitoba." *Canadian Perspectives*, Spring 2013, p. 19.

21. Katharina Frosch in Bollier and Helfrich, p. 226.

22. Mass Woods Forest Conservation Project. *The Outsmart Invasive Forest Species Project*. [online]. [cited October 22, 2013]. masswoods.net/outsmart.

23. Charles Schweik, Personal Communication, October 2, 2013.

Chapter 23: Re-enfranchising People as Commoners, Participants in Responsible Self-Governance

1. Charlotte Hess. "Mapping the Commons". Paper presented at the 12th Biennial Conference of the International Association for the Study of the Commons, July 2008. [online]. [cited November 29, 2013]. dlc.dlib.indiana.edu/dlc/handle/10535/304.

2. Bollier and Helfrich, , p. xiv.

3. Ostrom, *Governing the Commons*, p. 62.

4. Ibid., pp. 69–76.

5. Ibid., p. 101; Wagner, "Self-governance, polycentrism and federalism."

6. Ostrom, "The Future of the Commons," pp. 68–83.

7. R.H. Bates. "Contra Contractualism: Some Reflections on the New Institutionalism." *Politics and Society* Vol. 16 (1988), p. 399.

8. *We Rise Up* Video Documentary. Directed by Franziska Von Rosen. Produced for and available from The Grand Council of the Crees (gcc.ca);

Matthew Coon Come. "Building Strong Businesses on Firm Political Foundations." Speaking notes to National Conference on Indigenous Self-Government, Unuvik, NWT, September 10–12, 2013. (Available from GCC office).

9. Tom Nesbitt. "One Trail: Facilitator's Report on the Sahyoue and Edacho Directions-Confirming Workshop." November 8–10, 2005. Available through Parks Canada; Morris Neyelle, Personal Communication.

10. Gibson-Graham, p 188.

11. Shrikrishna Upadhyay. "Community Based Forest and Livelihood Management in Nepal" in Bollier and Helfrich, pp 265–270.

12. Ibid, p. 267.

13. Diane Touchette, Personal Communication, November 21, 2013.

Chapter 24: The Commons as Culture, Community and Creation

1. Blomley, "Enclosure, Common Right," p. 320.

2. See The Cosmic Mass website. [online]. [cited November 30, 2013]. thecosmicmass.com; Adam Bucko and Matthew Fox. *Occupy Spirituality: A Radical Vision for a New Generation.* North Atlantic, 2013, p. 74.

3. Adams, p. 75.

4. Bucko and Fox, p. 59.

5. Tom Sherwood. "Religion and Spirituality in Student Life" in Trevor Kerry, ed. *International Perspectives on Higher Education: Challenging Values and Practice.* Continuum, 2012, pp. 69–86.

6. Bucko and Fox, p. 73.

7. Capra, *The Tao of Physics*, p. 68.

8. Matthew Fox. *A Spirituality Named Compassion.* Inner Traditions, 1999, pp. 88 (Eckhart) and 149.

9. Ronald Dworkin. *Religion Without God.* Harvard, 2013, Chapter One. Quoted from excerpt in *New York Review of Books*, April 4, 2013, p. 68.

10. Bucko and Fox, pp. 46 and 56.

11. Christine Boyle. "The United Church Diaspora." *The United Church Observer*, April 2013.

12. Atleo, *The Principles of Tsawalk*, p. 85.

13. Bearskin, Personal Communication.

Chapter 25: Common-Good Governance Locally and Globally

1. George Lakoff. *Moral Politics: How Liberals and Conservatives Think*, 2nd ed. University of Chicago, 2002, pp. 33 and 212–18.

2. Ibid., p. 212.

3. Ibid., pp. 215–16.

4. Workers' Solidarity Movement. "Occupy Movement, the Zapatista's and the General Assemblies." [online]. [cited November 30, 2013]. wsm.ie/c/occupy-movement-zapatistas-general-assemblies.

5. John Gaventa. "Global Citizen Action: Lessons and Challenges" in Michael Edwards and John Gaventa, eds. *Global Citizen Action*. Lynne Rienner, 2001, p. 278.

6. Benjamin M. Friedman. "'Brave New Capitalists' Paradise': The Jobs?" *The New York Review of Books*, November 7, 2013, p. 75.

7. "Harper's Index." *Harper's Magazine*, July 2013, p. 13.

8. Diana Bronson, Personal Communication, June 19, 2013.

9. Rick Sawa, Prince Albert Chapter, Council of Canadians, E-mail to Author, August 26, 2013.

10. Polanyi, p. 54.

11. McKibben, *Eaarth*, p. 105.

12. Adrian J. Randall. "The Philosophy of Luddism: The Case of the West of England Woolen Workers, ca. 1790–1809." *Technology and Culture*, Vol. 27#1 (January 1986), pp. 1–17.

13. Rebick, "Another U.S. is Happening!," pp. 305–314.

14. Peter Landre and Lester Travis. "Collaborative Watershed Management in the Finger Lakes Region, New York." Paper presented at Crossing Boundaries, the Seventh Biennial Conference of the International Association for the Study of Common Property, Vancouver, British Columbia, Canada, June 10–14, 1998. [online]. [cited December 8, 2013]. http://dlc.dlib.indiana.edu/dlc/handle/10535/1566.

15. Maude Barlow. *Our Great Lakes Commons: A People's Plan to Protect the Great Lakes Forever*. Council of Canadians, 2011.

Acknowledgments

First, I want to thank Betsy Nuse, the painstaking, astute and deft editor of my manuscript, as well as Ingrid Witvoet and the creative and promotional staff at New Society Publishers for believing in this book and bringing such talent to its completion.

I also wish to gratefully acknowledge the City of Ottawa and the Ontario Arts Council for grants that supported me while I wrote this book. For advice, information and other support in getting the content of the book right, I wish to thank the following scholars and researchers: Richard Atleo, Nicholas Blomley, Chris Bisson, John Buschek, Nick Card, Anne Carroll, Susan Buck, Irene Guijt, Tim Ingold, Jeanette Neeson, the late Elinor Ostrom, John Ralston Saul, David Geoffrey Smith, Clare Thomas and Jonathan Watkinson. Then there were others whose assistance was invaluable, including Margaret Archibald, Tracey Cooper, Libby Gunn, John Jack, Pat Kipping, Allan Leslie and Tommy Pringle. I want to thank the reference and access service staff at the Carleton University Library for their generous help in my research, Alasdair MacMhaoirn for his time helping me understand sometimes arcane Gaelic terms, Gail Martin for her work on the family geneology, Chris Bisson and Julia Cipriani for extra research assistance and Morning Star Woman (Bev Lubuk) for some gentle spiritual guidance. For generous hospitality and welcome in Scotland, I am grateful to Vivia and Allan Leslie, Joyce and George Moore, Jane and Kevin Ramage, Janet Sommerville, Clare and Anthony Thomas. I am hugely grateful to the members of the Covenant Team at the Gabriola Commons (Virginia Hayes, Judith Roux, George Szanto and K. Louise Vincent), for what I learned from our discussions, and for their friendship. I am thankful too for the love, faith and stalwart support of my friends, including Julia Cipriani, Rita Donovan (with special thanks for the Scots Dictionary), Sandy Duncan, Farhat Rehman, Margaret Singleton, Elaine Taylor, Bessa Whitmore and the late Chris Clark. Last but not least: thanks to my son, Donald Noble Burton, who has cheered me on throughout.

Index

About the Author

HEATHER MENZIES is an award-winning writer and scholar and the author of nine books, including *Whose Brave New World?* and *No Time*. She has been awarded an honorary doctorate and also the Order of Canada for her "contributions to public discourse." A mother and grandmother, a gardener and social justice activist, Heather regularly contributes to journals and newspapers and is in high demand as a speaker.

PHOTO BY RICHARD KERR

If you have enjoyed *Reclaiming the Commons for the Common Good* you might also enjoy other

BOOKS TO BUILD A NEW SOCIETY

Our books provide positive solutions for people who want to make a difference. We specialize in:

Sustainable Living • Green Building • Peak Oil
Renewable Energy • Environment & Economy
Natural Building & Appropriate Technology
Progressive Leadership • Resistance and Community
Educational & Parenting Resources

For a full list of NSP's titles, please call 1-800-567-6772 *or check out our website* at:

www.newsociety.com

new society
PUBLISHERS